*Toward a Twenty-First Century
Biblical, Apostolic Church*

Toward a Twenty-First Century Biblical, Apostolic Church

A Critique of the New Apostolic Reformation Church in North America

SUYEON YOON
Foreword by R. Daniel Shaw

☙PICKWICK *Publications* • Eugene, Oregon

TOWARD A TWENTY-FIRST-CENTURY BIBLICAL, APOSTOLIC CHURCH
A Critique of the New Apostolic Reformation Church in North America

Copyright © 2019 SuYeon Yoon. All rights reserved. Except for brief quotations in critical publications or reviews, no part of this book may be reproduced in any manner without prior written permission from the publisher. Write: Permissions, Wipf and Stock Publishers, 199 W. 8th Ave., Suite 3, Eugene, OR 97401.

Pickwick Publications
An Imprint of Wipf and Stock Publishers
199 W. 8th Ave., Suite 3
Eugene, OR 97401

www.wipfandstock.com

PAPERBACK ISBN: 978-1-5326-5179-3
HARDCOVER ISBN: 978-1-5326-5180-9
EBOOK ISBN: 978-1-5326-5181-6

Cataloguing-in-Publication data:

Names: Yoon, SuYeon, author. | Shaw, R. Daniel (Robert Daniel), 1943-, foreword.

Title: Toward a twenty-first-century biblical, apostolic church : a critique of the New Apostolic Reformation Church in North America / SuYeon Yoon ; foreword by R. Daniel Shaw.

Description: Eugene, OR : Pickwick Publications, 2019 | Includes bibliographical references.

Identifiers: ISBN 978-1-5326-5179-3 (paperback) | ISBN 978-1-5326-5180-9 (hardcover) | ISBN 978-1-5326-5181-6 (ebook)

Subjects: LCSH: Apostolate (Christian theology). | Church polity. | Gifts, Spiritual. | Apostles. | Prophets. | Church renewal.

Classification: BV601.2 .Y66 2019 (print) | BV601.2 .Y66 (ebook)

Manufactured in the U.S.A.   SEPTEMBER 16, 2019

Dedication

To Jesus Christ
who is, who was, and who is to come, the Almighty

Contents

Acknowledgments ix
List of Tables xi
List of Figures xii
List of Abbreviations xiii
Foreword by R. Daniel Shaw xv
Introduction xix

PART I *Biblical Overview of Apostleship and its Ministry*
1 The Understanding of Biblical Apostle and Biblical Ecclesiology 3
2 Biblical Ecclesiology in the NT Church 30
3 Defining and Critiquing the Work of C. Peter Wagner
  and Other Proponents of the New Apostolic Reformation Church 47

PART II *Case Studies*
4 Study Methodology of Selected New Apostolic Reformation Churches 75
5 Case Study One: Manna Church 80
6 Case Study Two: Word of Life Church 101
7 Case Study Three: Bethel World Outreach Center 121
8 Findings from Case Studies 136

PART III *Moving toward a Biblical Church
in North American Context with a Broader Perspective*
9 Ecclesial Elements and Church Growth in North America 151
10 Ecclesial Elements in the Broader Context:
   Emerging and Missional Church 167

Recommendations 181

Contents

Appendix A	An Inquiry about "Apostolic Church Case Study" 187
Appendix B	Case Study Cite: A Letter from C. Peter Wagner 188
Appendix C	Record of Data for Semi-Structured Interviews 189
Appendix D	Interview Questionnaire for Manna Church 193
Appendix E	Interview Questionnaire for Michael Fletcher of Manna Church 194
Appendix F	Interview with Mel Mullen 195
Appendix G	Interview with Word of Life Church 196
Appendix H	Interview with Rice Broocks 197
Appendix I	Interview Questionnaire For Bethel World Outreach Center 198
Appendix J	Interview Assessment 201

Bibliography 203

Acknowledgments

When I began this doctoral program, I thought I was pursuing just a PhD degree in a quest to get a teaching job. However, in the end, I realized a shift in my lifestyle and perspective from slumber in research to a research-oriented mentality. In other words, this research process has reshaped me as a whole. Many people helped me as I struggled through this transformation process, resulting in this book.

Eddie Gibbs has been most influential to me, empowering me towards being an authentic researcher. He challenged me from the very start of the process, biblically critiquing my data from time to time and thus setting for me a pattern to follow.

Daniel Shaw, my chair, has been more than just my chairperson in that he has been an encourager and a true supporter throughout the program. When I faced serious financial difficulties, he was the one who opened the door for me to continue my research. Most of all, he ensured the harmony of my research as he believed in me as well as in other committee members.

Ryan Bolger provided sharp and cutting-edged comments each time I missed the big picture. He truly brought timely valuable inputs, which led my thoughts into a clear direction.

I give special thanks, from the bottom of my heart, to Douglas Pennoyer, an outside reader. He gave vital feedback on my book with heart-felt encouragement.

I owe a lot to Joel Green. His contribution on Part I, biblical exegesis, became the backbone of analyzing my data. He gave the best whenever I asked numerous references for the New Testament study.

I also would like to recognize the three apostles from my case studies. They graciously opened up their stories for me to gather necessary data. Without their generosity, I could not have been able to do this valuable study.

Acknowledgments

My family was there for me always. I drew a lot of strength from them when I felt like I had no energy to keep myself going. My mother is a prayer warrior who supported me with unceasing intercessory prayer. My late father was a friend in my heart who stimulated my soul into creative thinking. My brother's life as a medical-missionary challenged me always to strive for the best in my own life. My sister's warm mind was there for me when I needed emotional comfort.

My friends are a vital part of this process. I thank Grace and Joseph for their endless kindness, Pastors John and Michele's prayers and encouragement, Junia and Todd's timely comfort have been so helpful to me; I will never be able to repay their sacrificial support during my research.

List of Tables

Table 1   Critique-Framework for Apostle   15
Table 2   Critique-Framework for Biblical Ecclesiology   44
Table 3   Critique of the Definition of Apostleship in NARC   54
Table 4   Critique of the Role of Apostleship in NARC   57
Table 5   Critique of the Concept of Apostleship in NARC   58
Table 6   Data Collection   79
Table 7   The Gap Between Ideal and Reality in Case One   98
Table 8   Between Ideal and Reality in Case Two   117
Table 9   The Gap Between Ideal and Reality in Case Three   133
Table 10   Indicators of Apostleship from the Case Studies   137
Table 11   Indicators of Ecclesiology from the Case Studies   141
Table 12   Comparison of the Three Movements   177

List of Figures

Figure 1 Overlapping Roles and Ministries 41
Figure 2 Flow Chart of Data Analysis 77
Figure 3 Moving Toward Biblical Ecclesiology 176

List of Abbreviations

BWOC   Bethel World Outreach Center
NARC   New Apostolic Reformation Church
WOLC   Word of Life Church

Foreword

R. DANIEL SHAW

SERMONS EXPOUNDING THE APOSTLE Paul's well known discussion of roles within the church in Eph 4:11–13 abound. But what did Paul mean by "Apostle"? Furthermore, how does the New Apostolic Movement at the beginning of the twenty-first century understand this biblical concept and Paul's injunctions about it? The contrast between biblical expressions of roles as intended by Paul's injunction to New Testament church congregations and how The New Apostolic Movement has positioned itself squarely behind the leadership of its foremost "Apostle", C. Peter Wagner provides an interesting case study that Dr. Yoon develops in this book. The contrast between biblical principles and practical manifestations within the movement, particularly as reflected in the definition of an Apostle, are stark and clear. With the Bible in one hand, and her research on the Movement in the other, Yoon clearly critiques this movement and subsequently compares it to similar contemporary manifestations in Conciliar and Evangelical Churches embroiled in cultural change. She creatively demonstrates how the Apostolic Movement is for contemporary Pentecostal churches what the Missional movement is for Mainline churches and the Emerging Churches are for Evangelicalism. Thus the development of the New Apostolic Reformation Church (NARC) as an ecclesial Movement provides a dynamic case study to reflect on the meaning of "Apostle" in the biblical sense, while critiquing a contemporary Charismatic environment as it develops beyond the vision of its now deceased founder.

Yoon's research design is well thought out and her research carefully executed, focusing on three case study churches in three different regions of North America: Western Canada (Alberta), the Eastern Seaboard (North Carolina) and the Deep South (Tennessee). Based upon interviews and participant observation in the three representative contexts, Yoon describes the leadership and ecclesiology based on descriptions from the members themselves. This enables her to subsequently demonstrate the gap between the biblical and conceptual ideals and the reality of ecclesial practice. This allows for comparison of similarities and differences as it pertains to the demographics, ecclesiology, church dynamics and the gap between Apostolicity, as established through biblical exegesis, in contrast to principles Wagner laid out. The cultural diversity of her respective case studies clearly demonstrates core, non-negotiable, themes within the movement while recognizing these themes play out in the reality of individual congregations within their contemporary contexts.

The book is well structured with a focus on biblical background, processing the nature of apostolicity in Scripture and in the context of the New Testament Church in Part I. In Part II she lays out her research carefully presenting her methodology followed by the three case studies as well as a careful comparison of her findings across the corpus. This leads to Part III where she notes the characteristics of Church Growth principles from Wagner's earlier writing and teaching as they apply to his newer approach to developing the NARC. The resulting structures within the Pentecostal Movement bear resemblance to what has happened in both the Conciliar Movement and the Evangelical Churches of North America. She concludes the book with recommendations and application to relevance in the North American context.

The value of this book is the position Yoon takes to the movement she describes and critiques. As a Korean woman in the North American environment, her work is by definition cross-cultural. This gives her a perspective from which she is able to critique the North American Church environment, thereby pointing out culturally induced blind spots. She recognizes the role of culture on the socio-dynamics of church growth in North America while pointing out that it may be different were these churches in another part of the world. Furthermore, as a woman she brings a gender role to her study that reflects concerns males may not identify. Her careful research, reading, and awareness of the ecclesiastical issues in North America lead her to make a valuable contribution both academically and in terms of ethnographic presentations of church. She discovers that the biblical role of an apostle is to make the church missional by emphasizing the "sending-concept", whereas Wagner focused on the apostle as a church leader. This contrast enables her to evaluate the three case study

Foreword

communities as they represent, to various degrees, the NARC Movement. Such analysis demonstrates that each apostolic community is different from the others, as well as from the biblical and conceptual ideals. Yet, together they are all part of the NARC, thereby allowing for critique of the Movement.

Yoon's work is proving to have long-term implications for the NARC since Wagner's death. Her important conclusion is that the NARC serves as a charismatic manifestation comparable to what has happened in other ecclesiastical manifestations in North America. She sees the Apostolic Movement as a response to culture change within a long-standing Pentecostal tradition extending back to Azusa Street. Similarly, other churches are also navigating these complex waters and adjusting structures along with manifestations that extend their reading of biblical principles into contemporary North American culture. The NARC, Yoon argues, is a cultural adjustment that requires a new reading of the role of an Apostle within the Pentecostal environment. This important socio-religious insight makes this book a worthy contribution to the ecclesiological literature as well as for the NARC as a movement among Pentecostals in particular and North American ecclesiology in general.

As you read, I encourage you to pay attention to the creative methodologies Yoon employed as she adapted her research tool to meet the needs of each community she spent time in. Note how she juxtaposes biblical exegesis and socio-religious research in order to understand cultural manifestations in light of biblical expectations. It is this attention to place in the broader context of biblical understanding that enables Dr. SuYeon Yoon to make a valuable contribution to the dynamics of a socio-religious movement. This book makes a missiological as well as ecclesiastical contribution that will serve both communities well.—enjoy the read and apply the principles to your own ecclesiastical environment.

R. Daniel Shaw
Sr. Professor of Anthropology and Translation
Fuller Graduate School of Intercultural Studies
Pasadena, California
December 15, 2018

Introduction

> I urge you to live a life worthy of the calling you have received. Be completely humble and gentle; be patient, bearing with effort to keep the unity of the Spirit through the bond of peace. There is one body and one Spirit—just as you were called to one hope when you were called, one Lord, one faith, one baptism; one God and Father of all, who is over all and through all and in all. It was he who gave some to be apostles, some to be prophets, some to be evangelists, and some to be pastors and teachers, to prepare God's people for works of service, so that the body of Christ may be built up until we all reach unity in the faith and in the knowledge of the Son of God and become mature, attaining to the whole measure of the fullness of Christ (Eph 4:1–6, 11–13, NIV).

ACCORDING TO THE APOSTLE Paul, each member of the body of Christ has a divine calling—called to be apostles, prophets, evangelists, pastors, and teachers to prepare God's people for works of service. When we, as Christians, are prepared for works of service, our lives reflect our calling.

I grew up in Seoul, Korea, and rarely heard of homeless people because in the 1970s and the early 1980s, our culture was so closely structured around the family unit. I remember the first time I saw a homeless person on the street one rainy morning in 1978. When I came close enough to see her face, my throat tightened and my eyes got teary. Then, I said to myself: "I can't believe this is a human being!" She looked like an animal that had been thrown out into the street and left to die! I wondered what had happened to her and what went wrong with her family.

Today, when I study modern missional ecclesiology, I am often reminded of that frightful sight and feeling I had back in Korea when I saw that homeless woman. From one perspective, that homeless woman serves as a metaphor for the church. Even though she was a human being, she didn't look like one. Furthermore, she could not function as a human being to pursue a purpose and be treated as a human. Likewise, if the church does not appear as it should due to the fact that it is institutionalized and fragmented, it will not function in the way God intended. Just like that homeless woman, the church will no longer be recognized as the church by outsiders.

In this study, I envision a biblical church in the twenty-first century North American context. In order to arrive at this vision, I will critique the New Apostolic Reformation Church (NARC) in two distinct ways: (1) in the light of biblical inspiration on apostolic leadership and missional ecclesiology, and (2) in the light of its contemporary application in the NARC. Furthermore, I will stress the need for the NARC to be a biblical church in a broader context. Both the Emerging Church and the Missional Church will serve as the broader context for the NARC to pursue a biblical Ecclesiology in the twenty-first century.

Background

I have been part of a para-church movement, as well as cross-cultural missions, in local churches throughout Asia, Central America, and the United States. As a Korean-born fourth generation Christian, one of the most significant influences on my spiritual formation has been the authoritative church environment of the Asian culture. However, my international, intercultural, and interracial experiences outside of Korea shifted my perspective of the church from being merely in the context of a particular location to a universal perspective. Recently, my ministry has been focused on developing leaders, transforming communities, and reaching out to non-believers, as part of a team.

During the past seven years with the NARC, I have pioneered as a student-volunteer, engaging in campus evangelism on both high school and college campuses in the San Gabriel Valley, empowering and equipping members of the younger generation to serve on "apostolic teams" and to encourage some to become teamwork-oriented leaders.

Even though ministry with the NARC has enhanced my understanding of church development, it has been a struggle to find how this movement fits into the broader body of Christ in terms of missional ecclesiology. This book is my first step in compiling case studies of NARCs, which will attempt to generate a theological conversation with other missiological movements. Three NARCs served as the case studies for my field research, which enabled me to explore spiritual, theological, missiological, and theoretical implications.

Furthermore, this research serves as the initial consideration in my being able to develop an understanding of the twenty-first century Biblical Apostolic Church. The contributions of this book will sharpen missional and biblical ecclesiology for the twenty-first century North American context.

Purpose

The purpose of this study is to identify biblical ecclesiology within the NARC in the North American context in order to critique NARC through an understanding of biblical principles and reflect on other missional movements that may serve as examples of missional ecclesiology for the NARC. I seek to draw out principles that reflect the NARC's ecclesiological contribution to the broader body of Christ.

Goals

The ultimate goal of this study is to apply my critique of the NARC to actual case studies in order to foster biblical ecclesiology within the NARC and to contribute the apostolic emphasis of the NARC to the broader body of Christ.

Significance

I anticipate that this research will make at least two significant contributions. First, it will supplement my future professional goal of helping the NARC to explore the transferability of early church life to the present day. Secondly, this will add to research archives on the Apostolic Church development, which has not yet been evaluated from a biblical and ecclesial perspective due to its newness. As post-modern churches are going through "the greatest change in the way of doing church since the Protestant Reformation,"[1] a research that positions this new movement into the structure of the entire body of Christ and highlights its apostolic influence on the twenty-first century North America church is of critical importance.

1. Wagner, *Churchquake*, 8.

This understanding will enhance the effectiveness of missions in NARCs in the twenty-first century.

Based on my findings, I will make recommendations pertaining to a biblical framework for a biblical NARC. The biblical understanding of NARC will enhance the broader effectiveness of being a Missional Church in North America. Understanding the biblical framework for an Apostolic Church contains a broader significance in that it enables me to contribute to the missional objectives for the manifold ministry of Christ and his church.

Central Research Issues

The central research issue is to determine biblical values that critique ecclesiology of the NARC and compare it to other missional movements in the North American context.

Research Questions

1. What are the missional considerations that shaped the first century ecclesiology, as revealed in biblical sources?
2. How do biblical criteria of ecclesiology influence ideas and values relating to New Apostolic Reformation manifestations in North America?
3. What is the ecclesiology of the New Apostolic Reformation Church in North America today?
4. Are there significant correlations between the rise of emerging and missional movements and the rise of the NARC?
5. How can churches in the twenty-first century become more biblical?

Definitions

Apostle: One who is called and sent by Christ having the spiritual authority, character, gifts, and abilities to advance God's Kingdom on earth.

New Apostolic Reformation Churches: Churches that recognize and relate with modern-day apostles within the New Apostolic Reformation Movement.

Introduction

Post-modernity: A recent emerging cultural and historical period that is characterized by the reversal of modern values.

Biblical Ecclesiology: Biblically developed ecclesiology from the first century church and echoed to us today primarily through Ephesians 4:11–16 and 1 Corinthians 14:1–26.

Delimitations

First, I selected Apostolic Churches as defined by C. Peter Wagner.[2] Secondly, this research focuses only on the NARC in the context of North America, not the world as a whole. Thus, the contribution of this research may not be directly applicable to NARCs in other cultures. Thirdly, my intention is not to explore the dynamics between the NARC and the postmodern cultures, rather I intend to enhance a biblical ecclesiology in the North American churches. Lastly, my findings on the NARC are based on my working experience in three NARCs in the North American context. This implies that my findings can be verified with other samples.

Assumptions

1. I assume that the gift of apostle was never designed to cease; it was intended to be a perpetual gift throughout the church age.
2. I assume that the development of the NARC in North America is strongly influenced by C. Peter Wagner.
3. I assume that a biblical ecclesiology is to "become mature, attaining to the whole measure of the fullness of Christ" (Eph. 4:13).

Overview

This book is structured in three parts. In Part I, I survey a biblical understanding of ecclesiology. In Chapter 1, I exegete the biblical passages to establish the criteria for a critique of apostleship within NARC. In Chapter 2, I establish criteria for critique of missional ecclesiology within NARC. In Chapter 3, I define and critique the work of Wagner and other proponents

2. Wagner, *New Apostolic Reformation Church*.

of the NARC's understanding of an apostle and apostolic ministry in light of biblical studies, church history, and its contemporary application in the NARC.

In Part II, I examine three NARCs based on my critique in Chapter 3 beginning with introduction of methodology of the three case studies in Chapter 4. From Chapter 5 to Chapter 7, I present the data from three NARCs and describe their leadership and ecclesiology based on their own description. In the presentation of data, I include the critique of their theory as well. The critique is separated into two parts; one is the gap between the biblical perspectives and the NARC's own perspective, and the second is the gap between theory and practice. I present each case study, Chapter 5, Chapter 6, and Chapter 7, in a similar way, which, in turn, highlights how different each one is from the others. Yet, together they are all part of the NARC, thereby allowing for critique of the movement. Chapter 8 summarizes my findings from the three case studies.

In Part III, I seek to explore the broader church context in North America by providing a survey of the current church atmosphere in regards to areas of ecclesiological development in a complex, contemporary environment. In Chapter 9, I discuss issues around the distinctive marks of the church, asking questions such as: "What really makes the church the church?" and "Are we forming ecclesiology as Jesus would?" In Chapter 10, I observe the fruits of ecclesiological factors manifested in the Emerging and the Missional Church movements, which parallel the NARC. I argue that Emerging and Missional Churches are creating a *kairos* moment in North America that will eventually produce a relational structure for church communities that can appropriately reflect and relate to contemporary cultures in ecclesiology.

Part I

Biblical Overview of Apostleship and Its Ministry

Part I formulates a biblical reference from which to critique the NARC in general and the case studies of Part II in particular. Here, I survey a biblical understanding of apostle and biblical ecclesiology as the criteria for a more in-depth critique of the NARC.

Chapter 1

The Understanding of Biblical Apostle and Biblical Ecclesiology

IN THIS CHAPTER, I discuss the definition of being 'sent' and its usage in relation to an apostolic mission. There are two different parts to this discussion; the Understanding of Apostleship in the New Testament, and the Biblical Ecclesiology in the New Testament Church. Note should be taken that my intention in this chapter is not to discuss apostolicity in relation to the Catholic notion of apostolic succession from the Apostle Peter through an unbroken line of bishops, nor the pre-reformation and Protestant tradition.

Understanding of Apostleship in the New Testament

I briefly survey the definition of apostleship by reviewing the origins of the apostle-viewpoint and how the apostle was perceived in the New Testament. The first part of this discussion, the origin of the apostle-viewpoint, is found in three different places: In the Old Testament (OT) and rabbinic Judaism, in secular Greek, and in Gnosticism. The second part of the discussion, the perspective of apostle in the New Testament, includes: The Twelve, a Synoptic understanding of apostleship, a Pauline understanding of apostleship including exegesis of the Pauline biblical texts, and looking at Jesus as an apostle. Finally, I create a table for critique framework for an apostle summarizing a discussion of the understanding of apostleship in the New Testament (NT).

Origin of the NT Apostle-concept

In this part, I discuss the origin of the apostle-viewpoint in chronological sequence from the OT and rabbinic Judaism, NT Greek context, and in Gnosticism.

From Old Testament and Rabbinic Judaism

Similar to the classical literature usage of *apostolos*, the apostle-viewpoint in the NT has its origin in the usage of the term apostle as "a figure of late rabbinic Judaism [designated as] *saliah*, sent man."[1] The apostle-viewpoint, *saliah*, is summarized as *saliah*-convention in the rabbinic period. The viewpoint of this *saliah*-convention is, however, secular and legal. The significant evidence shows a link between "the verbal use of the root *saliah*," and "the use of *apostellein*."[2]

Even though J. B. Lightfoot[3] was the first to draw the relationship between the NT apostle and *saliah*, according to Francis H. Agnew, K. H. Rengstorf brought an in-depth understanding by clarifying the *saliah* as the "sending-convention" in relation to the NT *Apostolos*.[4] To confirm Rengstorf's claim, the Talmud describes *saliah* as a commissioned agent, or one sent to act in the name of another.[5] Repeating Agnew's view of the sending-convention in the rabbinic Judaism, J. Andrew Kirk also brought attention to the term *shaliah* as an ambassador and the pre-Christian Jewish representative.[6] This *saliah*-sending-convention is significant for the Christian apostolate in terms of distinguishing the sender and the sent.

Agnew carefully points out that the context of "sender and sent" lies in a legal convention, not a religious convention.[7] Because this *saliah*-convention is a legal one, the sender refers to a human sender, meaning that it is hard to ascribe God as a sender in this legal convention.[8] In addition to Agnew's reservation, Kirk rejected and criticized the work of Rengstorf and

---

1. Agnew, "Origin of the Apostle-Concept," 79.
2. Agnew, "Origin of the Apostle-Concept," 84.
3. Agnew, "Origin of the Apostle-Concept," 76.
4. Agnew, "Origin of the Apostle-Concept," 79.
5. Agnew, "Origin of the Apostle-Concept," 80.
6. Kirk, "Apostleship Since Rengstorf," 250.
7. Agnew, "Origin of the Apostle-Concept," 81.
8. Agnew, "Origin of the Apostle-Concept," 81, 86–87.

others who conceptualized "*saliah*-sending-convention," noting that it is "lacking both in concrete evidence and in intrinsic probability."[9] Regardless of lack of evidence, lack of intrinsic probability, and little connection with religious convention, a strong link was made by Rengstorf between the *saliah*-figures and the Christian apostle by tracing the roots to the *saliah*-convention in the OT and Rabbinic tradition. The strong link between the *saliah*-figures and the Christian apostle was supported in texts like John 13:16: "Amen, amen I say to you, a servant is not greater than his master or a messenger [*apostolos*] than the one who sent [*tou pempsantos*] him." In addition to John 13:16, the sent men of the community are found in both 2 Corinthians 8:23 and Philippians 2:25.[10]

In Secular Greek

The usage of the terminology "apostle" in secular Greek can be summarized largely in two different meanings: "messenger" and "sent."

First, in relation to the meaning of "messenger," Agnew confirms that, in secular Greek, the word *apostolos* is used twice in the book of Herodotus in likeness to the term "messenger."[11] He also stresses that the word *apostolos* is used here in a secular, non-biblical, Greek context that has no relation to the Christian usage. In addition to the usage in secular Greek and based on Agnew's research, the LXX and Symmachus repeat the word *apostolos* to imply "messenger."[12] Thus, this cannot be related to the origins of Christian usage.

Secondly, in relation to the meaning of apostle as "sent," D. Muller and F. Graber note that both *apostello* and *apostolos* are both used to designate an apostle in classical literature.[13] Graber explains that the term *apostello* is a compound of *stello*, which means 'to put up, or make ready,' and the preposition *Apo*—that is, from, away, back—means "send, send away, chase away, send off." A technical term denotes the divine authorization.[14] Along with Graber's definition, C. G. Kruse confirms *apostello* as meaning "sending of

---

9. Kirk, "Apostleship Since Rengstorf," 251.
10. Agnew, "Origin of the Apostle-Concept," 84.
11. Agnew, "Origin of the Apostle-Concept," 75.
12. Agnew, "Origin of the Apostle-Concept," 75.
13. Graber and Muller, "Apostle," 127.
14. Graber and Muller, "Apostle," 127.

persons with a commission and a divine sending and authorization."[15] According to Kruse, the term *Apostolos* has two ideas of usage: an expression commissioning and being sent overseas. Kruse added that *apostolos* was used in reference to "the dispatch of an army and then in reference to the army itself."[16] That means that *apostolos* in the classical literature was used as either an "authorized agent" or "having been sent."

In Gnosticism

In contrast to the legal and secular convention of *saliah*, W. Schmithals argues that the apostle-viewpoint deviated from Gnosticism.[17] A more restricted use of the term "apostle" likely represents a safeguard against certain Gnostic claims. In the third part of his work, Schmithals makes a clear distinction between the heavenly redeemer-figure and the earthly redeemer-figure.[18] His main point is that the Gnostic earthly-redeemer figure is similar to the Christian apostle, which can be described as "a member of the community of the spiritual."[19] He added several commonalities between the earthly-redeemer figure and a Christian apostle, including that they undertake a worldwide mission.[20] The highlight of his contribution is defining *apostolate* as an appropriation of the missionary office of Jewish or Jewish-Christian Gnosticism, suggesting that the Christian apostle-viewpoint came from the early Christian experience or a form of Gnosticism.[21]

The Definition and Role of Apostle in the NT

The origin of the apostle-viewpoint provides a strong perspective for the word apostle: "messenger," "sent," and "missionary figure." Regardless of the fact that the theory of the origin of apostle-viewpoint has been tested and rejected by later scholars, the core presentation of each viewpoint has been contributed in terms of defining the word, *apostle*. Speaking from the

15. Kruse, "Apostle," 27.
16. Kruse, "Apostle," 27.
17. Agnew, "Origin of the Apostle-Concept," 88.
18. Agnew, "Origin of the Apostle-Concept," 88–89.
19. Agnew, "Origin of the Apostle-Concept," 89.
20. Agnew, "Origin of the Apostle-Concept," 89.
21. Agnew, "Origin of the Apostle-Concept," 90.

origin of the apostle-viewpoint, I will provide the definition, the role, and the concept of apostle in the NT by discussing four distinctive perspectives: the Twelve, a Synoptic understanding of apostleship Pauline-apostleship, and Jesus as an apostle.

The Twelve

The Christian usage of the word *apostolos*, based on Agnew's research, can be discovered in the NT eighty times.[22] His research shows that the term *apostolos* is used throughout the NT books, specifically in the Pauline epistles (thirty-five times), and thirty-four times in the gospel of Luke.[23] New Testament scholars have conducted extensive research on the apostleship concept since 1865, beginning with the work of Lightfoot. Lightfoot opened up the "veritable flood of literature," according to Agnew.[24]

However, the common conclusion about the "veritable flood of literature" cannot define the usage of the word *apostolos*. Agnew concludes that the broadly approved characteristic of the apostle can be described as: "One who, through a vision of the risen Lord, has become an official witness to his resurrection and who has been commissioned by him to preach the gospel in a way fundamental to its spread."[25]

Agnew drew this conclusion by referring to other scholars, R. E. Brown and F. Hahn. Brown affirms the characteristics of "a vision of the risen Jesus," and "a commission by Jesus to preach," as being "an apostle of Jesus Christ."[26] Following Agnew's conclusion and Brown's affirmation, the criteria of apostleship is strictly limited to Jesus's Twelve. Kirk also discussed the criteria of apostleship[27] as identical to Agnew's:

- Apostles must be witnesses to the resurrection of Jesus Christ.
- They must be witnesses to the earthly life of Jesus.
- They must be called either by the earthly Lord, the risen Lord, a Christian congregation or any combination of the three.

---

22. Agnew, "Origin of the Apostle-Concept," 84
23. Agnew, "Origin of the Apostle-Concept," 84.
24. Agnew, "Origin of the Apostle-Concept," 76.
25. Agnew, "Origin of the Apostle-Concept," 77.
26. Agnew, "Origin of the Apostle-Concept," 77.
27. Kirk, "Apostleship Since Rengstorf," 255.

- They must be faithful to their unique ministry.

Kirk clarified the criteria of apostleship with respect to the nature of apostleship (2 Cor 1:1) and a special charisma such as performing miracles, suffering, and teaching.[28] Apostleship means that the calling of an apostle is from God, 'an apostle of Christ Jesus by the will of God.'

Everett Ferguson also defines two distinctive usages of the word "apostle."[29] He concludes that the New Testament usage of the word "apostle" refers to "the twelve disciples specially chosen by Jesus" (Luke 6:13–16; Matt 10:1–4; Mark 3:14–19; Acts 1:13f) and to Paul (Gal 1:1; Rom 1:1; 1 Cor 15:9). He stresses that the criteria for being an apostle are:

- to be personally chosen by Jesus,
- witnesses of his resurrection—except Judas (Acts 1:21–26), and that
- by their testimony and work of planting churches, they formed the foundation of the church (Eph 2:20; Rev 21:14).

Hans Dieter Betz shows that Luke only identifies the Twelve as Apostles (Matt 10:1–2; Mark 3:14).[30] Jesus appointed his Twelve, gave them "authority" over the demons, and sent them to preach (Mark 3:14; 6:30). Betz explains extensively the concept of Jesus' Twelve as Apostles by looking at Luke's understanding of the Twelve Apostles. He identifies and limits apostleship solely to the Twelve Apostles.[31]

Ferguson agrees with Betz that subsequent Christian literature used "apostle" more broadly than the NT and changed the meaning more to that of being a missionary. The first group of missionaries was the seventy who were sent out by Jesus (Luke 10:1) and the second group consists of the "apostolic men" who are associates of the Twelve and Paul.[32]

Synoptic Evangelists' Understanding of the Apostolate

Although the overwhelming usage of "apostle" in the Gospels and Acts is a technical term for the Twelve and Paul, Ferguson provides a broader use

---

28. Kirk, "Apostleship Since Rengstorf," 256.
29. Ferguson, "Apostle," 72.
30. Betz, "Apostle," 310.
31. Betz, "Apostle," 310.
32. Ferguson, "Apostle," 73.

of "apostle" which does not limit the circle of apostles to the time of Paul, but rather, to a wider usage than that of the Twelve. Evidently, Paul himself reinterprets Luke's concept of the Apostles as he rejects the criterion, "having known the historical Jesus personally" (2 Cor 5:16), but stresses the criteria as "witnessing the resurrection" (Gal 1:16; 1 Cor 9:1–5; 15:1–10), and "founding churches" (Rom 11:13; cf. 1:5–7; 13–15).[33]

C. G. Kruse states that, "Jesus called apostles" (Matt 4:18–22; 9:9; Mark 1:16–20; 2:14; Luke 5:1–11; 27–28) is one of the firm common elements to all the Synoptic evangelists. The verses indicate that Jesus chose the Twelve for a Galilean mission initially so that he could also involve the Twelve in a Galilean mission while they accomplished their mission in his name.[34] His emphasis lies in the task of an apostle, indicating that the apostleship of the Twelve is distinctive in terms of their unique mission.

Kruse takes his point further to refer to Matthew 28:18–20, where the emphasis is on the nature of the apostolic task:

> All authority in heaven and on earth has been given to me. Therefore go and make disciples of all nations, baptizing them in the name of the Father and of the Son and of the Holy Spirit, teaching them to observe all that I have commanded you; and behold, I am with you always, to the close the age. (Matt 28:18–20)

Green states that as a gospel writer, Mark focuses not so much on the task of the apostles, but on "the universal nature of the apostolic commission and on the serious implications of people's response to the apostolic message based on Mark 16:15–16."[35]

Similar to Matthew, Luke stresses the role of apostles as being "witnesses to the death and resurrection of Jesus Christ and to the call for repentance and offering of forgiveness in his name."[36] In John, Jesus highlights an extension of his ministry to the Twelve after his resurrection, "Peace be with you. As the Father has sent me, even so I send you" (John 20:21).

In short, Synoptic Evangelists described an apostle as a missionary, or "apostolic men." Synoptic Evangelists provided grounds for the wider use of "apostle" than merely constrained to the Twelve, Paul, or even the Seventy.[37]

---

33. Agnew, "Origin of the Apostle-Concept," 77.
34. Kruse, "Apostle," 32.
35. Green and McKnight, *Dictionary of Jesus and the Gospel*, 33.
36. Green and McKnight, *Dictionary of Jesus and the Gospel*, 33.
37. Kirk, "Apostleship Since Rengstorf," 256.

Pauline Usage of Apostleship

Betz made an important distinction between Paul and the Twelve in terms of their unique mission. According to Betz, the Twelve Apostles are "the leaders of the Jerusalem church and Paul as apostle of the Gentiles."[38] He states that Paul attempts to be the same as the Twelve (1 Cor 15:3–10), yet later he uses the word apostle for himself (Phil 1:1; 2:25; 1 Thess 2:7). Paul struggles, however, with his apostleship until his death (Col 1:24), he clearly rejected the criterion for apostleship as to knowing the historical Jesus personally (2 Cor 5:16). According to Betz's distinction between Paul and the Twelve, Paul was qualified as apostle by founding churches (1 Cor 15:10) and by being an apostle to the Gentiles (Rom 11:13). The summary of Betz's criteria of Paul's apostleship is:

- not appointed by human authorities (Gal 1:1, 12, 15, 16) but by the risen Christ himself, either personally or by revelation
- witnessing the resurrection (Gal 1:16; 1 Cor 1–5; 15:1–10)
- founding churches (1 Cor 15:10).[39]

Kirk made points relating to Betz's criteria. He asserts that Paul's understanding of apostleship lies strongly in the task of church planting.[40] He states, "Paul's apostleship is proved, not by any exclusive claim, but by the fruits of those who exercise it."[41]

If Kirk's interpretation is true, that the Twelve were distinct in their "unique and unrepeatable function to fulfill" and that they "fade from the picture once the Gentile mission is under way,"[42] then the continuity of apostleship depends on the nature of the apostolic calling, including the concept of what it means to be 'sent ones.'

With that in mind, going back to the discussion of the Christian apostle-convention, I will summarize by stating that the obvious characteristics of Paul's apostleship are: prophetic vocation, messenger or accredited representative, specially recognized early Christian leader, and an apostle to "build-up the church."

---

38. Betz, "Apostle," 310.
39. Betz, "Apostle," 310.
40. Kirk, "Apostleship Since Rengstorf," 261.
41. Kirk, "Apostleship Since Rengstorf," 261.
42. Kirk, "Apostleship Since Rengstorf," 261.

Prophetic Vocation

It is worthwhile to reflect on the purpose of the previous discussion of the *saliah* figure, earthly redeemer figure, and *saliah*-convention to define the understanding of a NT apostle. Schmithals's position, which considers the Jewish-Christian Gnostic's understanding of *saliah* to be analogues with apostleship as a religious phenomenon, was widely criticized and rejected by later scholars. Although there are objectionable differences between the commissioned apostle and the commissioned *saliah*, his main contribution remains.

In recent research, the discussion has moved from the *saliah*-convention and Christian apostle-convention to the word group *slh/apostellein* and NT apostleship.[43] The *saliah*-convention emphasizes the 'sent men' compared to the OT usage of *saliah*, which represents the prophetic sending of an apostle. Gerhardsson states that *slh/apostellein* is often associated with the word *nabi/prophetes* in the OT.[44] This suggests that the prophetic vocation of a NT apostle makes him a more significant figure than that of a sent-man figure.

In addition to Gerhardsson's understanding of the prophetic vocation of NT apostleship, he is supported by Hahn, who also gives attention to the word group *apostellein/pempein*, which means *slh* in OT usage.[45] Hahn goes on to stress Paul's own description of his prophetic vocation. Both Gerhardsson and Hahn emphasize the prophetic vocation of NT apostleship even as they try to give attention to the relationship between NT apostleship and the word groups "*slh/apostellein*" and "*nabi/prophetes*"[46]

In conclusion, in the light of *slh/apostellein* and *nabi/prophetes as* discussed above, one fact is evident; that Paul understood his apostleship, according to Agnew, "in terms derived from [an] OT description of prophetic vocation."[47]

---

43. Agnew, "Origin of the Apostle-Concept," 94.
44. Agnew, "Origin of the Apostle-Concept," 95.
45. Agnew, "Origin of the Apostle-Concept," 95.
46. Agnew, "Origin of the Apostle-Concept," 95.
47. Agnew, "Origin of the Apostle-Concept," 95.

Messenger or Accredited Representative

In addition to the linguistic understanding of apostleship in the NT, Paul's text itself testifies to his understanding of apostleship. In Paul's letters, the word *apostolos* appears thirty-four times identifying the title for himself as well as the Twelve. His use of *apostolos* can be summarized into two categories: a messenger, and a group of specially-recognized leaders in the Early Church Movement.[48]

Making reference to Paul's use of "messenger" or "accredited representative," Robert L. Plummer brought attention to the verses in 2 Corinthians 8:23, and to Philippians 2:25. After carefully examining the use of *apostolos* in the context of the Herodotus and Koine time periods, he firmly concludes that a "messenger" or "envoy" is Paul's primary use and understanding of apostleship in his letters.[49]

Specially-Recognized Early Christian Leaders

As for Paul's understanding of apostleship and the apostolic mission, Plummer distinguishes the apostolic office and the apostolic mission as unique from one another.[50] He views 1 Corinthians 9:1; 15:7–9 as referring to apostles as eyewitnesses of Jesus' resurrection, and Romans 1:1; 1 Corinthians 1:1; 15:7–9; 2 Corinthians 1:1; Galatians 1:1, 12, 15–16; Ephesians 1:1; Colossians 1:1; 1 Timothy 1:1, 11 as referring to the commissioning by Jesus as the understanding of apostolic office. Plummer characterizes the apostle's mission in three different spheres as he highlights the fact that there are different aspects of the apostolic mission to consider. He draws a sharp distinction between the apostolic office, authority, and general task. The difference in each sphere sheds insight on further discussion.

Regarding the apostle's mission, Plummer describes the evangelistic task as the primary apostolic mission in Romans 1:1; Ephesians 3:2–7; 1 Timothy 2:7; 2 Timothy 1:10–11. At the same time he reminds us that the main goal for evangelism is to establish mature congregations, not to "garner superficial adherence to the gospel."[51] Plummer refers to W. P. Bowers's work to extend his own understanding of the Pauline mission. Bowers

---

48. Plummer, *Paul's Understanding*, 45–46.
49. Plummer, *Paul's Understanding*, 46.
50. Plummer, *Paul's Understanding*, 46.
51. Plummer, *Paul's Understanding*, 47.

confirms and stresses: "the maturing of those young congregations" is the part of Paul's missionary work that may be summed up as "fulfilling the gospel."[52]

Consequently, according to Plummer, the apostolic task to perform miracles is only "in confirmation of the gospel" as referenced in Romans 15:18–19; 2 Corinthians 12:12; and Acts 2:43.[53] The way he positioned "signs, wonders and miracles" is remarkable. He brings in Romans 15:18–19 and 2 Corinthians 12:12 to establish a divine purpose for performing "signs, wonders and miracles."[54] This suggests that the gospel is the matter of top priority, not that of performing signs, wonders, and miracles. The authentic position for signs, wonders, and miracles is the divine confirmation of the gospel.

"Build-up the Church" Apostle

One of the most significant characteristics of an apostle, according to Paul's understanding, is that an apostle is someone who "builds-up the church." When we link passages such as Ephesians 4:11–16 and 1 Corinthians 14:1–26, we can easily acquire Paul's manner of understanding the apostolic way as being to build up the church. Paul clearly explains that the equipping of the saints should be the work, not only of apostles, but of prophets, evangelists, pastors, and teachers as well. The detailed meaning of "building up" the church is to edify and instruct one another according to 1 Corinthians 14:1–26.[55] This is exactly how Paul speaks about the way to "build up":

> But speaking the truth in love, we must grow up in every way into him who is the head, into Christ, from whom the whole body, joined and knit together by every ligament with which it is equipped, as each part is working properly, promotes the body's growth in building itself up in love. (Eph 4:15–16)

Plummer provides additional passages for "building up" texts such as Romans 14:19; 15:2; 1 Corinthians 14:3, 5, 12; and Ephesians 4:29. In addition to Plummer's understanding of the apostolic mission for building-up the church, Kirk echoes Plummer's view when he summaries the definition

---

52. Plummer, *Paul's Understanding*, 117.
53. Plummer, *Paul's Understanding*, 47.
54. Plummer, *Paul's Understanding*, 107.
55. Plummer, *Paul's Understanding*, 117–19.

of an apostle.⁵⁶ He puts "build-up" in his own words: "church planting."⁵⁷ I now shift from the definition of apostle to understanding the role and gift of apostle in the biblical context.

In short, I will create a table which will serve as a theoretical construct. The theoretical construct is from the biblical understanding of apostle. I am establishing a clear theological argument in this chapter so that I have a firm rationale for further critique. Further critique on the New Apostolic understanding of an apostle is biblically based on an understanding of apostleship in the ecclesiology of the first-century formation of the church. These criteria will be a framework of critique on chapter 3, and the three case studies as presented in Part II.

Exegesis of Pauline Biblical Texts

In this portion of my book, I will present an exegesis of Ephesians 4:11–13. I chose this text from the NARC's best case⁵⁸ to look at the definitions of an apostle and the ministry of an apostle; Ephesians 4:11–13. The focus is not to do an exegesis on the whole portion of the passage, but rather to expound on issues around the role of an apostle and the ministry of apostle. In addition to Ephesians 4:11–13, I will insert a brief discussion on "First of all apostles" from 1 Corinthians 12:28 for the sake of sharpening the discussion of Ephesians 4:11–13.

---

56. Kirk, "Apostleship Since Rengstorf," 262.
57. Kirk, "Apostleship Since Rengstorf," 262.
58. See Wagner, *Changing Church*, 32–3, 167; *Churchquake*, 104–5, 108; *Apostles and Prophets*, 30; *Apostles Today*, 22; Eckhardt, *Moving in the Apostolic*, 44–50; *Leadershift*, 8–12; Cannistraci, *Apostles*, 29, 36–37, 82.

Table 1

Critique-Framework for Apostle

	Term	Author	Meaning	Bible reference
Definition	**Apostle**	**By**	**Origin of Apostle-viewpoint**	
In Secular Greek	Apostolos	Agnew	1. Messenger and sent	
	Apostello	D. Muller	2. Sending of persons with a commission 3. A divine sending and authorization	
	Apostolos	Kruse	4. Authorized agent 5. having been sent	
In OT and Rabbinic Judaism	Saliah	Lightfoot Rengstorf Kirk	6. Sent man 7. Commissioned agent 8. One sent to act in the name of another ambassador	John 13:16 2 Cor 8:23 Phil 2:25
In Gnosticism	Apostolate	Schmithals	9. Appropriation of the missionary office of Jewish	
Definition	**Apostle**	**By**	**NT**	
	Twelve	Agnew Kirk Brown Hahn Betz	10. One who, through a vision of the risen Lord 11. Has become an official witness to this resurrection 12. Who has been commissioned by him to preach the gospel in a way fundamental to its spread	2 Cor 1:1 Luke 6:13–16 Matt 10:1–4 Mark 3:14–19 Acts 1:13f Gal 1:1, Rom 1:1 1 Cor 15:9
	Apostolic men	Ferguson	13. Missionary 14. Apostolic men who are associates of the Twelve and Paul	Luke 10:1
	Apostolos	Plummer	15. A messenger 16. Accredited representative, envoy 17. Missionary who fulfilling the gospel	2 Cor 8:23 Phil 2:25 Rom 1:1 Eph 3:2–7 1 Tim 2:7
Role of	**Apostle**	**By**	**NT**	
	Twelve	Betz	18. By their testimony and work of planting churches, they formed the foundation of the church	Acts 1:21–26 Eph 2:20 Rev 21:14 Matt 10:1–2 Mark 3:14 Mark 6:30

Book of Matthew	Apostle	Kruse	19. Carrying Great Commission	Matt 28:18–20
Book of Mark	Apostle	Green	20. Preach the good news to all creation	Mark 16:15–16
Book of Luke	Apostle	Green	21. Witnesses to the death and resurrection of Jesus Christ, to call for repentance and offer forgiveness in his name	
Book of John	Apostle	Green	22. Doing extension of Jesus' ministry	John 20:21
	Apostle	Betz	23. Founding churches	Phil 1:1, 2:25
	Apostle	Kirk	24. Church planter 25. Build-up the church	Eph 4:11–16 1 Cor 14:1–26
Eph 4:11–13 and 1 Cor 12:28	Apostle	Talbert Fee Collins	26. One who has ministry that comes first, chronologically, for pioneering church 27. One who lays a foundation for the church	1 Cor 12:28 1 Cor 12:28
Concept of	**Apostle**	**By**	**NT**	
	Apostle	Betz	28. Not appointed by human authorities, but by the risen Christ himself, either personally or by revelation 29. Witnessing the resurrection	1 Thess 2:7 Col 1:24 2 Cor 5:16 1 Cor 15:10 Gal 1:1, 12, 15, 16 1 Cor 1–5
	Apostel-lein	Hahn	30. Prophetic vocation	
	Apostolos	Plummer	31. One who perform "signs, wonders and miracles" only for the divine confirmation of the gospel	2 Tim 1:10–11
Eph 4:11–13 and 1 Cor 12:28	Apostle	Talbert Fee Collins	32. A spiritual gift for the church (Apostle-concept) 33. A tool to equip the church (Apostle-concept)	Eph 4:11–13 1 Cor 12:28
	Jesus as Apostle		34. Incarnational-humble servant	

Table 1 shows thirty-four different definitions, roles, and concepts of an apostle in the New Testament. These thirty-four perspectives will serve as a boundary for identifying the definition, role, and concept of apostle within the NARC. In chapter 2, I deal with the issues around Biblical Ecclesiology.

My ambition here is to move beyond the definition of an apostle and the definition of the ministry of an apostle; I will pursue factors about the nature of the church and the purpose of the church. In chapter 3, I use it as a plumb-line with which to measure the application of NARC definitions of the apostle and the practice of apostolic ministry against the Scriptures.

The theme of Paul's letter to the Ephesians can be summed up as Paul's ministry to the Gentiles.[59] The authorship of Ephesians is debatable; however, it is widely suggested that the letter came from Paul. N. T. Wright strongly insists that if the reader understands "Paul's thought in the way I think we should,"[60] there's no doubt that this letter is written by him. Andrew Lincoln also dismisses the debate of authorship saying: "[It] did not seem to be weighty enough."[61] The letter was written in the early 1960s traced by the fact that Paul was in prison in 3:1 and 4:1.[62]

Ephesians, a letter to the church in Ephesus, falls into three parts: (1) Prescripts and thanksgivings from Ephesians 1–3, (2) paraenesis including exhortations to maintain church unity, practical injunctions, and exhortations about Christian living, and (3) postscript.[63][64] Lincoln reflects the writer's two major concerns based on the two parts. In 1:18, he simply states that the first part represents a reminder of the readers' calling: "that you may know what the hope of his calling is."[65] The second part is an exhortation to respond to the calling, also, referencing 4:1: "[I] exhort you therefore to lead a life worthy of the calling with which you were called."[66]

Paul expresses a life which is worthy of the calling with the imagery such as the architectural language of building, and biological figures of the body. F. F. Bruce observes Ephesians 4:13–16 is the main climax of the writer's expression. The writer puts "the measure of the stature of Christ's fullness" as the main concern for the Ephesians by using imageries with

---

59. Bruce, *Epistle to the Colossians*, 229.
60. Wright, *Paul for Everyone*, 4.
61. Lincoln, *Ephesians*, lx.
62. Carson et al., *Introduction to the New Testament*, 309.
63. Bruce, *Epistle to the Colossians*, 240–41.
64. Lincoln, *Ephesians*, xliii.
65. Lincoln, *Ephesians*, xxxvi.
66. Lincoln, *Ephesians*, xxxvi.

architectural and biological development.[67] The usage of imageries with architectural and biological development is related to Paul's view of the body of Christ. He understood the body of Christ as one, yet many parts, connected together like the human body.

Also in his letter to the Ephesians, Paul draws the reader's attention to the vital aspect of unity. There is no accident in the word choice and diction he chooses to use in Ephesians 4:4–6. Note Paul's emphasis on unity with his reminders of oneness within the body of Christ. He repeats with the words: "There is one Spirit, one Lord, one God and Father, one body and one hope, one faith, one baptism" (Eph 4:4–6). As such, there should be no reason for disunity within the body. Verses 4:11–13, therefore ensure the audience should not miss the writer's point that although there are many gifts in the church, the purpose of the gifts is for the unity of the church.[68] I will now turn to a phrase by phrase analysis of the Ephesians 4:11–13 text.

And It Was He Who Gave (Eph 4:11)

This statement clearly reveals the origin of gifts. Andrew Lincoln helps us to distinguish the word between "give" and "appoint."[69] The difference between give and appoint determines whether an apostle here is a gift or a position. Lincoln argued that Paul uses the word "give" meaning that an apostle is a gift to persons according to Jesus' will, not merely a position which is neither appointed nor created by the church. Charles H. Talbert draws from Harold Hoehner's[70] argument about gifts verses offices.[71] He explains that the list in Ephesians 4:11 is not about offices, but rather represents gifts to be bestowed upon the church. His point is clear that the offices of the early Christians were bishops, elders, and deacons, not apostles, prophets, and evangelists. The apostles, the prophets, the evangelists, the pastors, and teachers of Ephesians 4:11 are neither appointed nor elected.[72] He goes on to say the reason why these five gifts are mentioned here is was

---

67. Bruce, *Epistle to the Colossians*, 235.
68. Bruce, *Epistle to the Colossians*, 315.
69. Lincoln, *Ephesians*, 249.
70. Hoehner, *Ephesians*, 539.
71. Talbert, *Ephesians and Colossians*, 112.
72. Talbert, *Ephesians and Colossians*, 112.

to foster Christian unity within the church. Thus, he brought attention to the gifts, which are relevant for church unity.[73]

Later, Paul describes the very reason why the Lord gave people gifts: (1) so that the body of Christ can be built up by preparing people for works of service; and (2) that the body of Christ can be built up in unity, becoming mature to the degree of the whole measure of the fullness of Christ (Eph 4:13).

Ephesians 4:11 is actually connected with 4:10 in terms of linking "he" as the exalted Jesus who rules the universe. The intention of making this link is to recognize the church as a means to carry his purposes for the universe.[74] Lincoln goes on to make the point that when the readers come to an understanding of this, they also will better be able to position themselves to carry forward God's purposes for the universe. This provides a necessary perspective to the church as she builds herself up for a universal role and she regards her role to bring unity in Christ.

Some to Be Apostles (Eph 4:11)

Jesus gave "gifts" to the church including the gift of the apostle which was designed to be a tool to equip the people. He gave the gift of prophet, so that it would edify the church. Likewise, Christ gave the church the gifts of teacher, evangelist, and pastor all to equip the saints.

With regard to how God chooses people to be endowed with gifts for the church in various areas, there are no specific criteria or standards for the choosing method. God, in his sovereignty, chooses how people are to be gifted in the church. Every saint is considered equal in God's eyes. His ultimate purpose in bestowing gifts is to mature the church in its fullness and unity in the faith. The gift of apostle needs to be understood in the context of moving the church toward unity and maturity in the body of Christ (Eph 4:13). If there is no outcome of unity and maturity in the body of Christ, then, the gift of the apostle was in vain (Eph 4:12). In other words, the gift of apostle was given strictly for the unity and maturity of the body of Christ.

---

73. Talbert, *Ephesians and Colossians*, 112.
74. Lincoln, *Ephesians*, 248.

To emphasize the fact that Christ gave people as gifts to the church, Lincoln compares this part with Ephesians 4:7 and 4:8b that God gives not only grace to people, but also people to people.

He suggests the better translation of this part: "it was He who gave, on the one hand, the apostles, on the other, the prophets" or simply, as above: "it was he who gave the apostles, the prophets," rather than as in the most versions, "it was he who gave some to be apostles, some to be prophets."[75] This emphasizes that the writer's main concern was listing the nouns themselves. By doing so, Paul highlights the very things that the exalted Christ gives to the church; He gives people, these particular people who proclaim the Word and lead the church.

The five gifts can be separated into two different groups. The first three are the apostles, prophets and teachers. The apostles and prophets were singled out both in 1 Corinthians 12:28 and Ephesians 2:20. Lincoln reminds us that the roles of apostles are the commissioned missionaries and church planters. On the other hand, the prophets are specialists in mediating divine revelation.[76]

Unlike 1 Corinthians 12:28, the writer of Ephesians included two ministers in this part, the evangelists and the pastors. Lincoln makes an observation which is often overlooked regarding the reason behind mentioning the two categories of ministers here. He addresses the matter that the churches in Asia Minor might not have been pioneered by Paul, but rather by people such as evangelists and pastors or even Paul's co-workers and followers.[77] He explains this by observing how the evangelists were functioning in the post-apostolic period. According to Lincoln, it was the evangelists who continued to accomplish the mission of the apostles. Furthermore, he added, the pastors played a role in practicing his leadership in the church with the support of the teachers. It was, then, the prophet's role to work with the pastors. However, in the post-apostolic period, the role of pastor was shifted to co-labor with teachers in the leadership of church. That shift provided room for the evangelists to go for missions beyond the local congregation. Thus, based on Lincoln's argument, evangelists who are able to engage in the work of founding churches.[78]

---

75. Lincoln, *Ephesians*, 249.
76. Lincoln, *Ephesians*, 249.
77. Lincoln, *Ephesians*, 250.
78. Lincoln, *Ephesians*, 250.

Lincoln also highlights the qualities of teachers as they contributed their gift to helping the church to mature. They devoted themselves to the qualities of wisdom and knowledge to foster Christian norms and values as they "preserved, transmitted, expounded, interpreted, and applied the apostolic gospel and tradition along with the Jewish Scripture."[79] It was not just apostles and prophets who devoted themselves to bringing about church unity and maturity, but also the teacher's role to mature the church in the areas of wisdom and knowledge of the Son of God.[80]

First of All Apostles (1 Cor 12:28)

Lincoln uses 1 Corinthians 15:9 and Galatians 1:13 to analyze and indicate Paul's understanding of the church.[81] He points out that Paul uses two distinctive terms for "church" throughout his writings. One is for local assemblies of believers, and the other is for the universal church. C. Barrett verifies this by saying that apostles exercise their role in the universal church while prophets manifest their role in the assembly of the local church.[82] Because of Paul's view of the church, local assembly and universal, it is critical to clarify which one would be the case from the text.

According to James Dunn, in considering 1 Corinthians 12:27, "you are," Paul uses the word "church" to mean the church in Corinth which indicates the local assembly in Corinth.[83] Thus, most likely, the following instance, in 1 Corinthians 12:28, would be the church as the local assembly meaning that "first of all apostles" should be considered in the context of the local community.

Gordon D. Fee raised the question: "Does Paul intend that all of these be 'ranked' as to their role or significance in the church"?[84] He argued his case around the reason why Paul uses the word "first of all." Considering the fact that the first three ministries have precedence over the other, the

---

79. Lincoln, *Ephesians*, 251.
80. Lincoln, *Ephesians*, 251
81. Lincoln, *Ephesians*, lxiv, xciii.
82. Barrett, *First Epistle to the Corinthians*, 293.
83. Dunn and Donnelly, *Jesus and the Spirit*, 262–63.
84. Fee, *First Epistle to the Corinthians*, 619.

key is not arguing over the importance of gifts, but to highlight their role to found and build up the local assembly.[85]

Raymond F. Collins stands in a similar position to Fee in terms of his interpretation of "first of all" as a connotation of rank. Collins contrasts the idea of ranking gifts with Paul's understanding of apostleship. He explains that Paul's metaphor about apostleship can be described as someone who lays a foundation such as mother, father, and one who plants.[86] It means when we understand Paul's general view of apostleship, there is little room to mention "first of all" as superior status. He goes on to show how this ranking of gifts is unacceptable because Paul often uses words that describe his lower status in that community throughout his writing to humble himself; servants, workers, assistants, and stewards.[87] Clearly Paul portrays himself as of low esteem in the eyes of the world (1 Cor 1:20, 2:6, 9:16–19, 15:9).[88] Collins insists, furthermore, a foundational function of apostles by placing emphasis is on what apostles do: for an apostle, the focus is the preaching of the gospel, not the significance of the title.[89]

Richard B. Hays agrees with Collins and Fee that the itinerant apostle comes first in terms of building up the Christian community. He adds that the prophet and teacher come after the construction of the community and then continue in instructing the community.[90] He supports his argument with the fact that the rest of the lists, the workers of miracles, gifts of healing, helping hands, gift of administration, and speaking tongues (1 Cor 12:28), are not ranked in any hierarchical order.[91]

Lyle D. Vander Broek agrees with Hays. He puts the ranking of the first three gifts: apostle, prophet and teacher, as simply corresponding to their chronological appearance in the context.[92] This suggests that the role of apostle began very early at the start of the early church, and then the prophet and teacher appeared chronologically in succession. Anthony Thiselton

---

85. Fee, *First Epistle to the Corinthians*, 620.
86. Collins, *First Corinthians*, 468.
87. Collins, *First Corinthians*, 468.
88. Collins, *First Corinthians*, 468.
89. Collins, *First Corinthians*, 469.
90. Hayes, *Interpretation*, 216.
91. Hayes, *Interpretation*, 217.
92. Vander Broek, *Breaking Barriers*, 133.

also offers a similar evaluation to that of Vander Broek, the "threefold ministry as (one of) the primary (means of) Christian ministry."[93]

In short, "first of all" is seen in a chronological sense of the meaning, the role of laying the foundation of the community, and the apparent structure of the early Christian community. Thus, it is hard to regard "first of all" as the first rank but rather as a focus on key roles that serve to build up the local community of believers. There is no room to connect "first of all" with superiority in terms of authority. This conclusion goes well with the interpretation of "in the church" in the sense of the founding of the local church. The role of the apostle is the first in the series of appointments.

To Prepare God's People for Works of Service (Eph 4:12)

This part is related to how Jesus builds up his church. The body of Christ may be built up to prepare God's people for works of service. If saints were prepared for works of service, then it is a sign of the body of Christ being built. The goals for the preparation are unity and maturity.

It is very obvious that the writer gives reasons why he brings attention to different gifts. As we have learned above, the role of the apostle, prophet, teacher, evangelist, and pastor, each devote themselves to the church in a different manner and unique focus. As they give their own best from their gifts, according to Lincoln, the saints can play their role to build the body of Christ properly.[94] That was the process of "bring(ing) the saints to completion, for the work of service, for the building up of the body of Christ."[95]

His interpretation of Ephesians 4:12: "to prepare," is to complete and to restore God's people. Thus, the purpose of the gifts was clearly explained. The main purpose for gifts is to complete saints as they prepare themselves for "the ministries of proclamation, teaching, and leadership."[96]

So That the Body of Christ May Be Built Up (Eph 4:12)

This phrase clarifies the reason why people need to be prepared. Ultimately the preparation aims for the building up of the body of Christ. At the same

---

93. Thiselton, *First Epistle to the Corinthians,* 1014.
94. Lincoln, *Ephesians,* 253.
95. Lincoln, *Ephesians,* 253.
96. Lincoln, *Ephesians,* 254.

time, the purpose of Christ's gifts also can be defined as building up the body of Christ. For this reason, Lincoln discussed the issues of unacceptable self-glorification of having gifts. God gives gifts to be used in the church for the primary purpose of completing the saints for the building up of the body of Christ. There is no reason for ministers to be proud of their gifts.[97]

Until We All Reach Unity and Become Mature, Attaining to the Whole Measure of the Fullness of Christ (Eph 4:13)

The final outcome of the building up of the body of Christ is unity and maturity. In this passage, Paul tries to make clear that the edification of the body of Christ is not for the express interest of numerical growth of the church, but rather it is for Christians to develop maturity in the form of having the character of Christ. Also, Paul desires that Christians express unity in the form of oneness in mind and heart in the likeness of Christ.

As I mentioned earlier, the main focus of the ministries of pastor and teacher is to mature the body of Christ until it reaches unity in faith and in the knowledge of Christ as Lord. The goal is already set for us who are moving toward maturity and completeness. The moving force is contained in one faith.[98] Lincoln discusses the difference between the exercise of faith and content of that faith here. Because there was false teaching within the church in Ephesus, the writer was cautious about the teaching. Therefore, it is critical for the Church to stay in unity in the area of containing faith and knowledge.[99]

Summary

Following Talbert's analysis, this passage can be seen in three parts: (1) until we all attain unto the unity of the faith and of the knowledge of the Son of God; (2) unto a mature person; and (3) unto a measure of the stature of the fullness of Christ. The focus for the three parts is on inner growth of the church, not on the empowerment of missions.[100]

---

97. Lincoln, *Ephesians*, 254.
98. Lincoln, *Ephesians*, 255.
99. Lincoln, *Ephesians*, 256.
100. Talbert, *Ephesians and Colossians*, 115.

Lincoln also gives recognition to this view saying that in this phrase, Ephesians 4:11–13, understanding of the growth of the church lies with the church's inner growth rather than on its mission to the world.[101] F. F. Bruce also agrees with Lincoln when he concludes exegesis of v13 by defining spiritual maturity as "the measure of the stature of Christ's fullness."[102]

This discovery is fundamental to understanding the book of Ephesians as a whole. The five gifts, apostles, prophets, teachers, evangelists, and pastors, are for the saints' inner growth. The five gifts are not appointed by the church, but rather are bestowed by God. The five gifts are neither offices nor titles. The gifts were, in Ephesians 4:11–13, given for the purpose of spiritual maturity within the community of believers, not for the empowering of mission.

How, then, should I make the link between the biblical definitions of apostle in the previous section and the role of apostle as a gift from God to the church? Since the gift of apostle gave the church a means to find and build people to maturity in "the measure of the stature of Christ's fullness," the main focus of the apostolic position is to direct all saints to Christ. In doing so, the purpose of apostolic gifts will be fulfilled as well. In other words, the apostolic gifts in the local church will be fulfilled, in these particular verses, as the gift of the apostle contributes to the areas of the church's inner growth rather than contributing to the area of sending them to mission.

Rarely, do we find a case for the connection between the church's inner growth and, at the same time, fulfilling the Great Commission in the Bible. However, Luke inserts one scene from the time of Pentecost observed in Acts 2:47. "The Lord added to their number daily those who were being saved." The context was not the church doing mission. Rather, the people were fellowshipping with each other as they were gathering and sharing everything in common (Acts 2:42–47). They gathered together every day to devote to the apostles' teaching, to break bread, praise God, and enjoy the favor of all the people. The words here (1) devote, (2) praise, and (3) enjoy are more inward focused words than outward actions, indicating that they learned and practiced how to be united together as a community and by doing this they attracted new members, daily.

In support of this argument, Rodney Stark provides an insightful observation as he reports, "The basis for successful conversion movements is

---

101. Lincoln, *Ephesians*, 268.
102. Bruce, *Epistle to the Colossians*, 350.

growth through social networks, through a structure of direct and intimate interpersonal attachments."[103] The environment which consists of a walking distance life style and "undisclosed" openness made urban Christianity intimate. The small private places provided a social network system among urban Christians. As they share small space with each other, early Christianity grew as an intense community. He concluded the primary means of the early church's growth was "through the united and motivated efforts."[104]

Therefore the meaning of 'sent one' can be interpreted in conjunction with "the measure of the stature of Christ's fullness." It is fascinating to see how these two concepts come together in the sense that the exalted Lord who gives gifts to the church knows how to build a church in a way that mature people can be sent to the world, not only to do mission, but also to be missional.

Paul's intention in Ephesians 4:11–13 was not to address the Great Commission and missions per se; but rather, more accurately, Paul's primary reason for the existence of the distribution of gifts was for addressing Christians' inner growth, and spiritual vitality which would, then, enable spiritual reproduction. Also, it is an error to only hold the apostle responsible for the building up of the body of Christ—this responsibility belongs to all five gifts, not just to apostle. The evangelist, prophet, pastor and teacher are equally important in ministering to the church.

Jesus as Apostle

Mike Breen says, "Being 'sent' means being a part of God's apostolic mission—part of his desire to reach a lost world."[105] Breen believes the apostolic ministry is a continuation of carrying on Jesus' mission. Although apostolic teaching is clearly completed by the twelve disciples, the apostolic ministry, of being "sent out" to continue Jesus' mission of making disciples for the kingdom, has not yet been finished.[106]

Supporting Breen's belief in Jesus' apostolic mission, theologian C. K. Barrett made four simple points about identifying the marks of an apostle.[107] As John says, "You have not chosen me, but I have chosen you, and

---

103. Stark, *Rise of Christianity*, 20.
104. Stark, *Rise of Christianity*, 208.
105. Breen, *Apostle's Notebook*, 13.
106. Breen, *Apostle's Notebook*, 16.
107. Barrett, *First Epistle to the Corinthians*, 65–67.

I appointed you." C. Barrett shows that gracious, predestinating, divine choice is the first mark of an apostle. According to him, to "behold," "hear," and "obey" the words of Jesus are the other marks of being an apostle (John 15:16; cf. 6:70; 13:18).

C. Barrett also states that Jesus is the "starting point of apostolic ministry."[108] He continues to say: "Jesus is the apostle and high priest of our calling, and as such was the first 'sent one' . . . [thus, apostles] are 'sent' by God to bring his kingdom, share his gospel and build his church."[109]

Breen echoes C. Barrett when he tries to find validation for restoring the role of apostle in the present day by showing Jesus' ministry as apostolic ministry.[110] He suggests that Jesus was the pioneer in the characteristics of being an apostle; however, his assertion wasn't enough to close the current church debate about specific judgments having to do with restoring an apostle among the New Apostolic Reformation circle. He brings three passages from the New Testament to define Jesus' ministry as apostolic:[111]

"Now this is eternal life; that they may know you, the only true God, and Jesus Christ, whom you have sent" (John 17:3).

"From the days of John the Baptist until now, the kingdom of heaven has been forcefully advancing, and forceful men lay hold of it" (Matt 11:12).

"I will build my church, and the gates of Hades will not overcome it" (Matt 16:18b).

Breen summarizes the characteristics of Jesus' ministry as apostolic by defining its purposes: to advance the kingdom, to establish a new community, to rescue outsiders, and to develop the structures of a new corporate life for God's people:[112] pioneering, planting, bridging, and building.

Jesus, the apostle, pioneered by:

- Claiming lives as new territory for the kingdom of God
- Proclaiming the gospel to anyone who would hear
- Acting decisively with enemy counter-attacks
- Operating in divine authority and power

---

108. Barrett, *First Epistle to the Corinthians*, 13.
109. Barrett, *First Epistle to the Corinthians*, 13.
110. Breen, *Apostle's Notebook*, 40.
111. Breen, *Apostle's Notebook*, 37, 42–43.
112. Breen, *Apostle's Notebook*, 43.

- Establishing a bridgehead from which he could work.[113]

As an apostolic planter, Jesus:

- Recognized the right time to plant
- Identified the people who could open doors to other relationships
- Prioritized relationship over popularity
- Focused his energy and gifts into a small, gathered group
- Imparted a pattern of community life that could grow and multiply all by itself.[114]

As an apostolic bridge, Jesus:

- Recognized the different needs of diverse cultures
- Communicated appropriately according to cultural needs
- Used his pioneering and planting gifts to establish a cross-cultural bridgehead
- Addressed cultural prejudices among his disciples so that their eyes would be opened to the new bridging opportunity.[115]

As an apostolic builder, Jesus provided basic structures for the emerging community life of the church, including:

- Teamwork
- Shared life
- Common resources
- Repeatable teaching
- Strategies for mission.[116]

To summarize, it would appear that apostolic ministry:

- Is a call to pioneer a new frontier
- Is coupled with the provision of authority and power
- Comes with divine protection

---

113. Breen, *Apostle's Notebook*, 45.
114. Breen, *Apostle's Notebook*, 46.
115. Breen, *Apostle's Notebook*, 48.
116. Breen, *Apostle's Notebook*, 49.

- Requires submission
- Flows from weakness.[117]

The highlight from this section, Jesus as apostle, is to emphasize the incarnational aspect of his apostleship and that he operated as a humble servant.

---

117. Breen, *Apostle's Notebook*, 71.

Chapter 2

Biblical Ecclesiology in the NT Church

IN THIS CHAPTER, I will deal with the issues around the nature of biblical ecclesiology and the relationship between apostleship and biblical ecclesiology. Keeping in mind these issues, I will summarize the ecclesial elements of biblical ecclesiology in the NT Church, by which I may formulate a critique of the NARC. The focus of this summary will be drawn from the previous section "Definition of Apostleship in the New Testament."

Origin of the Greek

I will analyze two words which come from Greek origin to clarify the definition of the biblical church: *saliah* and *keryssein*. The word, *saliah* will help us to understand a church being missionary, and *keryssein* will assist us to understand preaching the gospel and healing the sick as an aspect of proclamation.

Saliah: Church Being Missionary

James D. G. Dunn discusses the significance of Jesus' teaching on the Kingdom of God.[1] He brings to the character of discipleship the question, "What did it involve to follow Jesus?"[2] In his book, the *saliah* principle (*saliah* = 'sent man') is defined as the root concept of apostleship.

---

1. Dunn, *Jesus Remembered*.
2. Dunn, *Jesus Remembered*, 543.

When Jesus called his disciples, the qualifications of being a disciple were to be able to learn from Jesus, to be "fishers of men," models of service, men of prayer, and prepared for suffering.[3] He successfully reflected the mission commission in both Matthew (Matt 10:40) and Luke (Luke 10:16). The words, "He who" and "him who sent me," emphasize the *saliah* principle of Jesus' mission. He made a clear note in "the *saliah* principle, that the one who is sent is as the one who sends, is generally understood to be at the root of the concept of apostleship."[4]

Furthermore, when John P. Meier symbolizes the Twelve as prophetic missionaries to Israel, Dunn's *saliah* principle becomes a necessary nature of the Twelve. However, for Meier the main focus of the "sending of the Twelve" is distinguished along with Dunn's *saliah* principle because the two share a basic common ground; sending missionaries.[5] Meier portrays the Twelve as prophetic: a symbol of the twelve tribes. He realized that the sending of the Twelve was a prophetic-symbolic action in the New Testament. The prophetic-symbolic action was actually the sending of the Twelve on a mission to Israel to anticipate the last day of God's re-gathered people.[6] Interestingly, he repeats Dunn's use of "fishers of men," particularly in the missionary call of the Twelve.[7]

Similar to Dunn and to Meier, Eckhard Schnabel holds that the *saliah* principle and prophetic missionary action are the core spirit of a "missionary commission" to the Gentiles.[8] When Schnabel speaks of taking the gospel to the Gentiles as the main ministry of Jesus, he brings attention to both the "preaching" and "healing" aspect of the gospel.[9] This "preaching" and "healing" commission is given to his disciples after his resurrection and can be found in Matthew 28:18–20, Luke 24:46–49, Acts 1:8, Mark 13:10, and John 20:21.[10] He ties the phrase of "[making] disciples" to the ecclesiological dimension of the mission of the Twelve. He strongly insists: "missionary work and church must not be separate, since the very goal and

---

3. Dunn, *Jesus Remembered*, 556–62.
4. Dunn, *Jesus Remembered*, 558.
5. Meier, *Companions and Competitors*, 154.
6. Meier, *Companions and Competitors*, 154.
7. Meier, *Companions and Competitors*, 161.
8. Schnabel, *Jesus and the Twelve*, 348.
9. Schnabel, *Jesus and the Twelve*, 325.
10. Schnabel, *Jesus and the Twelve*, 348–78.

purpose of missionary work is the creation of a community of disciples."[11] This indicates that making disciples is a visual demonstration of the purpose of the church: being missionaries. Thus, along with "making disciples" and "prophetic-missionaries," the *saliah* principle is one of the strongest characteristics of missional ecclesiology in the NT church.

Keryssein Mission

Luke 10:9 says: "Heal the sick who are there and tell them the Kingdom of God is near you." This was the missionary activity of his disciples, and likewise the missionary activity of the Missional Church through the ages. Meier contrasts two different groups around Jesus: his followers—the crowds, disciples, and the Twelve—and the other group, his competitors—the Pharisees, Sadducees, Esscenes and Qumranites, Samaritans, scribes, Herodians, and Zealots. He describes his competitors at length only to understand the reason why Jesus was creating new structures and a unique identity. Jesus' main vision was to restore meaning to his chosen people, to teach what it meant to be the true Israel:

> Reflecting Elijah's supposed mission of regathering the twelve tribes of Israel, Jesus created an inner circle of twelve disciples and sent them out on a mission to Israel. Like Elijah, Jesus was thought—even in his own lifetime—to have performed a whole series of miracles, including raising the dead.[12]

Meier repeats the idea that Jesus' purpose of calling his disciples was not merely to teach them the Torah, but for them to experience and proclaim the Kingdom of God.[13]

According to Schnabel, when the seventy-two disciples were sent out, the crucial strategy for the proclamation of the good news was to heal the sick.[14] The "preaching" and "healing" is the proclamation of the reign of God. *Keryssein* will be demonstrated as missional ecclesiology, which naturally ties in with the practice of "signs and miracles and wondrous deeds," which legitimize an apostle.[15]

---

11. Schnabel, *Jesus and the Twelve*, 356.
12. Meier, *Companions and Competitors*, 623.
13. Meier, *Companions and Competitors*, 55.
14. Schnabel, *Jesus and the Twelve*, 320.
15. Schnabel, *Jesus and the Twelve*, 290.

When Schnabel mentioned Jesus' mission to the Gentiles, he did not miss the unique method of proclaiming the good news to the Gentiles. Schnabel carefully and extensively layers stories about the centurion in Capernaum, the demon-possessed man in Gadara, the woman in Syro-Phoenicia, the deaf-mute man in the Decapolis, and the four thousand people east at the sea of Galilee as part of the evidence of Jesus' contact with Gentiles. Schnabel brought this evidence to light to prove his understanding of Jesus' mission to the Gentiles: that he both preached and healed.[16] This healing aspect, to Schnabel, must be included in terms of proclaiming the gospel. In other words, healing the sick is part of the gospel. Jesus performed healing miracles as he was proclaiming the reign of God to the Gentiles.

It was clear to Jesus that when he performed miracles, signs, and wonders, that He was to prophesy the rule and reign of God, not to demonstrate his own spiritual gifts, or to focus on his own spiritual authority. It is therefore noteworthy that his Elijah-like prophetic ministry was to expect the perfect Kingdom of God without sicknesses, suffering, or death. Thus, *keryssein* means to preach and to heal people for the sole reason of the reign of the Kingdom of God.

The Biblical Church Concept in the Early Church

David J. Bosch claims that 1 Peter 2:9 portrays the church as the one sent rather than the sender.[17] Bosch further describes the purpose of the church as being sent and building itself up for the sake of its mission.[18] His argument is based on his understanding of *Missio Dei*. He argued God as a missionary God, thus God's people are a missionary people.[19] Note that he warns about the difference between participation in the mission of God and missionary activities.[20] This means that the church needs to examine itself continuously whether or not what is being done is a participation in *missio Dei* or not. This way, the primary purpose of the *missiones ecclesiae* will be clear, namely:

---

16. Schnabel, *Jesus and the Twelve*, 333–40.
17. Bosch, *Transforming Mission*, 372.
18. Bosch, *Transforming Mission*, 372.
19. Bosch, *Transforming Mission*, 372.
20. Bosch, *Transforming Mission*, 391.

The primary purpose of the *missiones ecclesiae* can therefore not simply be the planting of churches or the saving of souls; rather, it has to be service to the *missio Dei*, representing God in and over against the world, pointing to God, holding up the God-child before the eyes of the world in a ceaseless celebration of the Feast of the Epiphany. In its mission, the church witnesses to the fullness of the promise of God's reign and participates in the ongoing struggle between that reign and the powers of darkness and evil.[21]

Actually, the discussion related to *missio Dei*, based on Bosch, is about missions. However, he sees the church as an instrument for God's mission. He indicates that the church needs to deliver God's mission not through doing activities, but rather by displaying the attributes of God.[22] The biblical church means, to Bosch, the church that is sent into the world in order to participate in God's mission by presenting God's attributes.

In addition to the concept of presenting God's attributes as an understanding of the mission of the early church, Bosch also emphasizes the reign of God as reflection on the biblical mission of the church.[23] He explains that to live under the reign of God within the covenant relationship with God (Gen15) was one of the missionary natures of Jesus' ministry.[24] Thus, to Bosch, the church should not only participate in God's mission, but also have a relationship with God as they live in his Kingdom now and in the future.[25]

With Bosch's biblical concept of the early church, the following section presents five different aspects of the early church: Breaking bread, Faith community, Holy Spirit centered, contains *oikos*, and Spiritual gifts.

Breaking of Bread

Rodney Stark claims that the rise of early Christianity occurred not because of mass conversions, but rather because of interpersonal relationships.[26] As Acts 2:41–47 states,

---

21. Bosch, *Transforming Mission*, 391.
22. Bosch, *Transforming Mission*, 390.
23. Bosch, *Transforming Mission*, 31–35.
24. Bosch, *Transforming Mission*, 32.
25. Bosch, *Transforming Mission*, 32.
26. Stark, *Rise of Christianity*, 20.

> Those who accepted his message were baptized, and about three thousand were added to their number that day [accepted the message and were baptized] . . . to the breaking of bread and to prayer. . . . All the believers were together and had everything in common. . . . Every day they continued to meet together in the temple courts. . . . They broke bread in their homes and ate together . . . and the Lord added to their number daily those who were being saved.

These are prime examples of the rich interpersonal relationships that the early church had. The early church experienced a phenomenal growth by breaking bread together, sharing their possessions, praising God, and enjoying the favor of all the people through the intimate organic relational network.

Wayne A. Meeks added that the benefit of paying attention to the social history is that we gain a perspective that helps us to understand the life of an ordinary Christian within that environment. The urban environment of the early church was comparatively smaller than in modern cities. Urban areas were small enough that a person could walk to the synagogue.[27] The city was an "undisclosed place"[28] rather than walled fortresses. Paul had "found" Priscilla and Aquila in some undisclosed place and he was introduced to their tent making workshop soon afterwards.[29] We can easily imagine that they walked together, talking and beginning to build their relationship. Lydia in Philippi (Acts 16:15), Jason in Thessalonica (Acts 17:5–9), Priscilla and Aquila in Corinth (Acts 18:2–4), Titus Justus, also in Corinth (Acts 18:7) all took up residence in these types of households.

In the words of Stark, "The basis for successful conversionist movements is growth through social networks, through a structure of direct and intimate interpersonal attachments."[95] The environment which consists of a walking distance lifestyle and "undisclosed" openness made urban Christianity intimate. The small private places provided a social network system among urban Christians. The function of a community and a social network are crucial factors for conversion. As they share small space with each other, recruits spring up from within and among their families and close friends.

In other words, once they were converted to Christianity, they typically turned to those with whom they had strong bonds. As a result of

---

27. Meeks, *First Urban Christians*, 26.
28. Meeks, *First Urban Christians*, 26.
29. Meeks, *First Urban Christians*, 26.

recruitment among those who shared an intimate relationship, early Christianity grew as an "intense community of believers." It grew not because of the miracles and credibility, but because of the invitation of breaking of bread and to prayer.[30]

Faith Community

The behavior of the early Christians clearly distinguished them from pagan's in the Greco-Roman world. The household congregations were related to each other in very intimate ways and interacted with each other very closely. They developed "a unique culture" by defining the language of belonging and the language of separating. They learned to distinguish themselves from "the outsiders" or the "unrighteous." There was compelling evidence from pagan sources that the "moral character [of] faith, hope, and love" were characteristic of Christian behavior.[31] Early Christianity revitalized life in the Greco-Roman world by providing people with a hopeful future, and helping people cope with many urgent urban problems such as epidemics, fires, and earthquakes. When crises came, Christians served one another and left a good impression on the pagans. Early Christians were able to cope with many urgent urban problems based on their steadfast faith for their future. They believed the promise, "Truly, I say to you, this generation will not pass away before these things take place" (Mark 13:30). They even faced death bravely. That kind of steadfast faith was significantly evident to others.

Conversion occurred by the survival rate as the Christians thrived, noticeably, through many disasters. Consequently, the early Christians survived substantially longer than pagans. Due to the attraction of survival rates, social networks shifted and a number of pagans came into Christian social networks.[32] The early Christians demonstrated their faith by their real lifestyle. The pagans made conversion decisions not based upon promotions of any "program," but rather by watching the lifestyle of Christians and desiring to be part of it.

---

30. Stark, *Rise of Christianity*, 208.
31. Stark, *Rise of Christianity*, 83.
32. Stark, *Rise of Christianity*, 75.

Holy Spirit Centered

In chapter 8 of Acts, Luke begins to introduce the geographical shift of the expanding Apostle's ministry. Right after the persecution, Philip carries his mission to the city of Samaria. This episode naturally connected to the next scene in "missions to the non-Jews." This opened the door for Peter to go to the Gentiles. One must pay close attention in how Luke's writing in Acts describes a shifting paradigm for the church. Luke's description in this chapter helps address questions of what is the agency of a shifting paradigm, and how these scenes help us in understanding the Missional Church.

Luke lays out the three-part structure of the book of Acts in 1:8, "You will receive power when the Holy Spirit has come upon you; and you will be my witnesses in Jerusalem, in all Judea and Samaria, and to the ends of the earth." This outline indicated the fact that the Holy Spirit empowered the early church in Jerusalem, then matured and transformed them in order to be effective in ministry to the ends of the earth.

The story of the Ethiopian eunuch foreshadowed the Gentile mission. Acts 1:8 recognized that you and I would be witnesses in Jerusalem, in all Judea, Samaria and to the ends of the earth. In this sense, the gospel will reach the ends of the earth. The definition of the people of God is overcoming the barriers and shifting the paradigm for the work of the Kingdom.

Even though Luke positioned the Holy Spirit as a main character in this narrative, he describes Philip as an active participant in his response characterized as "he started out" (Acts 8:27); "then Philip ran up to the" (Acts 8:30). The Holy Spirit took an initiative to create this scene; however, Philip also responds actively to carry out his mission. In light of verse 1:8 when Jesus told his disciples: "you will receive power when the Holy Spirit comes on you; and you will be my witnesses" the Holy Spirit was the cause of making one to be a witness. In fact, Philip did not choose initially to talk to non-Jews, but rather, the Holy Spirit led him to be a witness to non-Jews.

Luke strategically put this episode in the middle of a transition from Jerusalem to Samaria and Judea. Moreover, he did not highlight Philip as the main character of this scene. In the beginning of this scene, he started by using the word "Now" an angel of the Lord said to Philip right after Peter and John's ministry to the Samaritan villages. "Now" an angel of the Lord led Philip to an Ethiopian eunuch, non-Jews. It is not clear that we can call him a Gentile, but clearly, he was not a Jew. The Holy Spirit orchestrated Philip's ministry by demonstrating power through Philip in ministering to the Ethiopian eunuch in a powerful way. Philip opened up several conversations with the Ethiopian eunuch, led him to the Lord, and baptized him on the very same day.

It is very clear that the urgency of this event was not Philip, but an angel of the Lord and the Spirit of the Lord. When the Spirit of the Lord spoke to Philip, "he started out" and then "ran up," he did not know where he was going. "On his way," he met the Ethiopian. As noted in 1:8: "you will receive power when the Holy Spirit comes on you; and you will be my witnesses." Philip was moved by the Holy Spirit and became a mighty witness.

It is also important to note the sequential motif of "so" and "then" when an angel of the Lord began to move. When the Spirit moved, Philip responded to the Spirit. The Spirit of the Lord caused the event, and Philip responded to the Spirit. The role of the Holy Spirit in this episode can be described as a cause of the shifting Apostle's paradigm of ministering the "gospel to the Jews" to minister the "gospel to the non-Jews." Obviously, Philip had no idea of where he was going at the beginning of this episode. At the same time, he had no intention to bringing the gospel to the non-Jews.

In a nutshell, the audience of the book of Acts cannot but be drawn by the fact that following the Holy Spirit is the key to fulfilling the promise: "you will be my witnesses in Jerusalem, and in all Judea and Samaria, and to the ends of the earth." None of the Apostles had a strategy to be a witness to the ends of the earth. But it was the Holy Spirit that directed and enabled them in fulfilling this mission. The role of the Spirit is to fulfill God's sovereignty on earth.

Just as it was the case with the outpouring of the Spirit at Pentecost, Christians must seek the in-filling of the Holy Spirit in order to become freshly empowered for the ministry. The empowering of the Holy Spirit is the key for effectiveness in winning people to Christ. Robert L. Gallagher puts it this way: "The outpouring of the Spirit leads not only to the filling of the believer, but also to the overflowing of the Spirit to engulf those with whom he or she comes in contact."[33] Thus, he emphasizes the fact that the baptism of the Holy Spirit is an essential empowerment of the church evidenced by the speaking in tongues for a universal witness.

Containing *Oikos*

Based on Roger W. Gehring's research, a house church is a group of Christians that meet in a private home. A local church consists of all the

---

33. Gallagher and Hertig, *Mission in Acts*, 20.

Christians that gather at a geographically definable location. The terms "local church" and "house church" refer to the same group only if there is just one single house church gathering at that specific location. We will use the term "whole local church" or "whole church at one location" to refer to the whole church in one locality.[34]

The house churches in the early church played a missional role. The house churches were contained in an extended family called *oikos*. These *oikos* people, basically, were living their everyday life together, and gathering together to worship God. In the Jewish and Christian setting, domestic houses were viewed as "die urzelle der zusammenkunfte von Meister und jungern (the basic cell for the assemblies of the Master with his disciples)."[35] It is evident that Jews were accustomed to meeting for worship in the form of house synagogues and private homes—which was true for the early Christians as well. The house served as "fixed quarters for the missionaries, as a source for room and board, as a place for fellowship with new believers, and thus as a gathering place of the new faith community."[36] Moreover, Jesus and Peter used houses for the center of missional outreach.

Disciples planted house churches both in Jerusalem and beyond. Also, Paul planted house churches in the house of Lydia and in the house of the jailer. He was also extensively involved with mission outreaches in the cities of Thessalonica, Corinth, Ephesus, Rome, Colossae, and Laodicea using house churches as missional centers. In other words, one of the primary purposes of house churches was to operate as a missional base for the advance of God's Kingdom.

> Missional outreach began with a house, that is, with a family, which probably meant with the head of the household . . . the house and household were the immediate mission objective; the house fellowship was the starting and gathering point for the final objective, which was reaching the entire town or city.[37]

> This house is to become a starting point, a kind of headquarters, a center and base of operations for the following stage of the mission, reaching the entire town.[38]

---

34. Gehring, *House Church and Mission*, 27.
35. Gehring, *House Church and Mission*, 29.
36. Gehring, *House Church and Mission*, 60.
37. Gehring, *House Church and Mission*, 54.
38. Gehring, *House Church and Mission*, 55.

> Center mission implies a series of young congregations networked with and equal to one another in the cities, that is, centers, which then became bases of operation for the Pauline mission.[39]

The early churches essentially saw themselves as the "house of God." Within the "house of God," the elders and the leader of the household became the leader of the church. A leadership structure of the house churches was:

> Already in place from the very beginning, built into the social infrastructure of the ancient *oikos* in advance. . . . This is also a possible explanation for why leadership structures were already in place in Thessalonica after such a short time.[40]

The house church model can make a significant contribution in the industrialized countries of the West. The house church can provide a setting for "the opportunity in which personal encounters, human warmth, and trusting, long-lasting relationships can be experienced."[41]

Exercising Spiritual Gifts

Arthur G. Patzia claims that the early church operated under "the direct influence of the Holy Spirit and its members [exercised] their spiritual gifts for the common good."[42] This charismatic community exercised individual gifts for the common good of the body of Christ. The Twelve Apostles were recognized as the leaders of the early church until Paul and Barnabas's mission trip. The primary function of an apostle was to "be a witness to the gospel." Besides apostolic leadership, prophets, teachers, evangelists, deacons, elders, pastors, and women were significant components of the leadership in the early church. The function of the leaders interlocked and overlapped with each other rather than promoting distinct roles.

---

39. Gehring, *House Church and Mission*, 181.
40. Gehring, *House Church and Mission*, 201.
41. Gehring, *House Church and Mission*, 304.
42. Patzia, *Emergence of the Church*, 153.

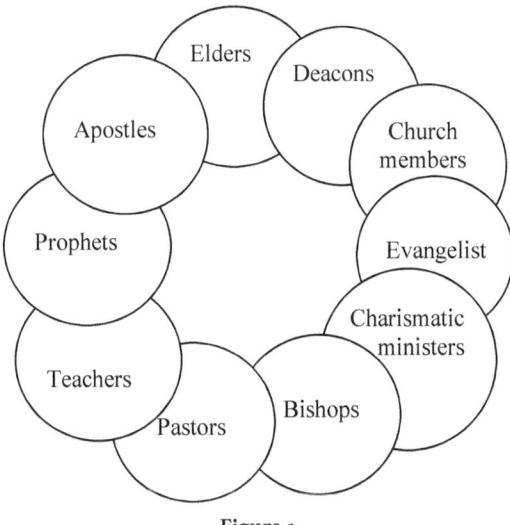

Figure 1

Overlapping Roles and Ministries[43]

The form of early Christian worship can be characterized by creeds, confessions, hymns, liturgical expressions, and sacramental acts. These diverse forms of worship developed within the structural organization of common households. Regardless of different forms of worship in the early church, the Holy Spirit often manifested within a worshiping community of believers.

The Biblical Church Concept in Paul's Understanding

Paul understood a Christian community as an open, dynamic, and caring communion. The community practiced fellowship through their gifts and ministries. That fellowship was vital for building up the community, and was also a key for bearing witness about God presence in the world. Paul often used metaphorical language like; agricultural, domestic, architectural, and somatic, to express his view of *ekklesia* and presented it neither in terms of hierarchy nor in terms of its mechanism.

---

43. Patzia, *Emergence of the Church*, 182.

Not Hierarchical, But Organic Community

For Paul, the community was "a loving family"[44] and at the same time, was "a functional body."[45] The terminology, "family," indicated the basis of the community as relational and organic, not mechanistic. When he saw a Christian community, he saw a beloved divine family who related to each other with familiar affection (1 Thess 3:12). The nature and exercise of gifts present in the community would be the key factor to understanding "a functional body." The primary implication of the functional body metaphor to the exercise of gifts is through the variety of contributions each has to offer.[46] It is very clear that Paul understood the Christian community as an organic loving family who distinguished themselves and related to one another through exercising their gifts. Therefore, the structure of a Christian community was neither hierarchically nor mechanistically organized.

Howard A. Snyder echoes the fact that the church should be structured organically, not hierarchically. He sharply contrasts the biblical DNA of the church and a cultural soil. He warns: "For Christians, this uncritical acceptance of the hierarchy is a problem. Hierarchy has been read into Scripture, Christian theology, and ecclesiastical structures for fifteen hundred years. Many Christians believe that the universe is hierarchical, that the church and the family are hierarchical institutions."[47] His point is that a family is neither hierarchical nor a vertical line, but a circle, emphasizing network or living organism character. He continues: "The New Testament does not teach hierarchy as the principle of either authority nor organization in the church."[48] When Paul is speaking of "first apostles, second prophets, third teachers" of 1 Corinthians 12:28, he indicates an historical sequence of how God planted the church, not a hierarchical order to run the church. The roots of hierarchy lie in cultural history and are not based on the Bible. The answer is very clear and simple: a biblical interpretation and ecclesiastical practice need to re-examine the issue of the hierarchical structure within the body of Christ.

If Snyder's analysis is true, then how can we possibly shift our paradigm from being hierarchical to being biblical? How should we transfer the idea of an organic family and loving, relational community to the present

---

44. Banks, *Paul's Idea of Community*, 47.
45. Banks, *Paul's Idea of Community*, 58.
46. Banks, *Paul's Idea of Community*, 61.
47. Snyder and Runyon, *Decoding the Church*, 106.
48. Snyder and Runyon, *Decoding the Church*, 108.

church setting? Learning from Paul, it would be very crucial to identify the gifts among the congregation. Then exercising gifts will help the church to overcome their hierarchical concept of understanding and relating to each other. For Paul, the word *"charismata"* expressed the basic principle involved in his approach to the dynamics of church.[49] The nature of the *charismata* can be described as open-ended in character, individual, not evenly distributed, ranked according to their benefits, regularly and occasionally contributed, not only new but renewed, and exercised on any appropriate occasion.

Equipping the Saints: Ephesians 4:11–13

Going back to the conclusion of my discussion of Ephesians 4:11–13 (see chapter 1), the indication of the Missional Church[50] can be described as a "church that equips God's people" (Eph 4:11–13). The aim is to equip the saints to attain to the whole measure of the fullness of Christ: inner growth. The understanding of the church in Ephesians 4:11–13 agrees well with Bosch's understanding of *missio Dei*. Both are emphases of the character of Christ and attributions of God as the growth of church or purpose of church.

Continuation of Jesus' Pioneering Mission: Acts 2:42–47

Reflecting on "Paul's understanding of apostleship" and "Jesus as an apostle," the word pioneer stands out. In terms of relating "pioneer" with ecclesial elements in the New Testament, Breen provides helpful insights. He says, "being 'sent' means being a part of God's apostolic mission—part of his desire to reach a lost world."[51] Breen confirms that the apostolic ministry is a continuation of carrying on Jesus' mission. Although apostolic teaching was completed by the twelve disciples, the apostolic ministry, to be "sent out as being [a] pioneer," that is, continuing Jesus' mission of making disciples of the kingdom, has not yet been finished.[52]

---

49. Banks, *Paul's Idea of Community*, 92.

50. The usage of "Missional Church" here means "church that equips God's people" as they focus on missional activity in contrast to its specific use as an approach and attitude of the denominational churches in response to *missio Dei* in Part III.

51. Breen, *Apostle's Notebook*, 13.

52. Breen, *Apostle's Notebook*, 16.

Supporting Breen's assertion of Jesus' pioneering mission, Martin Garner discusses the theological meaning behind the succinct statement: "understanding the gift and the role of apostle." He brings up points that reiterates the "sent one" side of Apostolic leadership in terms of "pioneering, breaking ground, [and going] with nothing."[53] Although he concludes his book with a prayer for more apostles to be raised up and released in the body of Christ, he recognizes the tension between "established boundaries of the local church" and "exercising apostolic leadership" in our current post-modern Christian context.[54] His main insight is to bring pioneering-apostleship into today's church in order to restore and enhance the purpose of the church. Without the pioneering-apostleship, the church cannot carry out its missional calling.

With the characteristic of missional ecclesial elements in mind, in the next chapter, I will seek to bring together a biblical understanding of the apostle as a tool for comparison and contrast.

My intention is to critique the New Apostolic Reformation Churches in North America in the light of a biblical understanding of apostleship and missional ecclesiology in the New Testament, in order to imagine what an authentic, biblical, twenty-first-century apostleship and Apostolic Church can look like. In other words, the measure of apostolic success will be considered within the context of the contemporary relevance of an apostle in the present-day context.

Table 2

Critique-Framework for Biblical Ecclesiology

	Term	Author	Meaning	Bible reference
Origin of	**Greek**	**By**		
Saliah	Sent one	Schnabel	1. Missionary work and church must not be separate 2. Make disciples	Matt 28:18–20 Luke 24:46–49 Acts 1:8, Mark 13:10 John 20:21
Keryssein	Proclaim	Meier Schnabel	3. Proclaim the Kingdom of God 4. Preaching and healing	Luke 10:9

---

53. Garner, *Call for Apostles Today*, 3–11.
54. Garner, *Call for Apostles Today*, 27.

Biblical	Church	By	NT	
1 Peter 2:9 and *Missio Dei*		Bosch Scherer	5. Participate in God's mission 6. Presenting God's attribution	1 Peter 2:9
Early church	Breaking bread	Stark Meeks	7. Intimate community	Acts 2:42–47
	Faith-based community	Stark	8. Faith community	Mark 13:30
	Holy Spirit centered	Fred Gallagher	9. Doing mission led by the Holy Spirit	Acts 1:8 Acts 8:1
	Containing Oioks		10. Inviting extended family into everyday life	
	Exercising Spiritual gifts	Patzia	11. Operated under the direct influence of the Holy Spirit	
Paul's understanding of church	Not hierarchical but organic	Banks Snyder	12. Loving family without hierarchical order 13. Organic family 14. Exercising gifts to hurdle the hierarchical concept of understanding and relating to each other	1 Cor 12:28
	Equipping Saints	Snyder	15. Equipping saints by using spiritual gifts	Eph 4:11–13
	Continuation of Jesus' Pioneering mission	Breen Garner	16. Sent out as being a pioneer 17. Breaking ground	Acts 2:42–27

I conclude this chapter with Table 2 which serves as a theoretical construct designed from the biblical understanding of missional ecclesiology. I established a clear theological argument in this chapter so that I have a firm rationale for further critique. Further critique on the New Apostolic understanding of an apostle is biblically based on an understanding of apostleship in the ecclesiology of the first-century-formation of the church. These criteria will be a framework for critique in chapter 3, and the three case studies as well.

Summary

In summary, the definition of the biblical church can be categorized by three different characteristics: (1) having continuity of Jesus' mission, (2) being a church that engages in mission, and (3) being a church that equips saints for the work of doing mission. The continuity of Jesus' mission is, based on Acts 2:42–47, to baptize people and to be obedient to the apostle's teaching which focuses on what apostles do and not on the office of the apostle.

In Act 2:42–47, though Luke does not specify what the teaching is, we can assume continuity with Jesus' teaching. In addition to the continuity of Jesus' mission, the biblical church is a church with outward focus and passion. The churches in the book of Acts and Paul's understanding of community demonstrate a church that is fully positioned and participating in God's mission in the world.

Lastly, according to Ephesians 4:11–13 and 1 Corinthians 12:28, the purpose of the biblical church is to prepare saints for the work of ministry by recognizing and using their diverse gifts. Again, the focus here is not the gift of apostle, but the work of an apostle to enhance all the saints' maturity and inner growth.

In the next chapter, I bring out point by point, the need for the NARC to be well positioned and participating in God's mission—preparing the saints for ministry as their theory says. This critique will enable NARC to envision a biblical understanding of being an apostolic church in the twenty-first-century North American context.

Chapter 3

Defining and Critiquing the Work of C. Peter Wagner and Other Proponents of the New Apostolic Reformation Church

IN THIS CHAPTER, I define the work of C. Peter Wagner, and critique his work as well as other proponents of the NARC understanding of apostle. The biblical framework for an apostle and for biblical ecclesiology, from the previous chapter, serves as a tool in this critique. The understanding of apostleship and biblical ecclesiology will set apart the "ideal" aspect of NARC from the "reality" aspect of NARC. The reality aspect of the NARC will be demonstrated in the three case studies of Part II.

Definition of Apostleship in the NARC

In 2002, Wagner stated, "This is my fifth book relating to apostles. In none of the first four did I offer a definition of an apostle."[1] Wagner never offered a definition of apostle up to that point because he said, "I was on such a rapid learning curve that I feared intuitively that any definition I came up with would probably soon have to be revised, perhaps many times over."[2] The fear that he perceived in 2002 was not the first time he faced it. He reminds us that when the term "evangelist" came out back in Charles Finney's time, 1825–1875, Finney had to expose himself to the theological argument in using "evangelist" as his title. Wagner concluded that this phenomenon of

1. Wagner, *Spheres of Authority*, 27.
2. Wagner, *Spheres of Authority*, 27.

controversy against calling one an "apostle" will eventually die down as was Charles Finney's case in the past.[3] In 2002, Wagner overcame his reticence to defining apostle and suggested the following:

> An apostle is a Christian leader, gifted, taught, commissioned, and sent by God with the authority to establish the foundational government of the church within an assigned sphere of ministry by hearing what the Spirit is saying to the churches and by setting things in order accordingly for the growth and maturity of the church.[4]

Similar to Wagner, Cannistraci defined an "apostle" as:

> One who is called and sent by Christ to have the spiritual authority, character, gifts and abilities to successfully reach and establish people in kingdom truth and order, especially through founding and overseeing local churches.[5]

His definition emphasizes the aspect of an apostle being an ambassador.[6]

Wagner, Eckardt, and Cannistraci are three main voices writing about the New Apostolic circle as they propose and explore the definition, role, and characteristics of an apostle. This shaping process continues today, as they rely on each other and allow others to shape their own explanations of what they propose. Wagner's understanding of apostolic leadership development is largely characterized by a shift in viewing the "apostle" first as a gift, then later as an office or title.

The Role of Apostle in NARC

The perspective of apostleship within the NARC went through changes from 1999 to 2002. The perspectives of apostleship were developed by Wagner, along with others from his apostolic network—most importantly, John Eckhardt and David Cannistraci. These authors quote from one another's writing, borrowing ideas and also receiving corrections from one another. I chronologically summarize these concepts of apostleship and its relevant roles within the NARC.

---

3. Wagner, *Churchquake*, 110.
4. Wagner, *Spheres of Authority*, 27.
5. Cannistraci, *Apostles*, 29.
6. Cannistraci, *Gift of Apostle*, 26.

Apostle as Warrior

According to John Kelly, the president of Leadership Education for Apostolic Development, the critical factor that distinguishes the New Apostolic Reformation Movement from the denominations is its church governmental structure and heavy dependence upon the function of apostles. He says: "Apostolic movement brings the church from a reactive mentality to a proactive mentality in the warfare of spiritual, political, economic and cultural dominion."[7] For him, the number one role of the apostle is doing spiritual warfare. He understands the five-fold ministry as: prophets, pastors, evangelists, and teachers are to help an apostle to get his job done. The apostle is, eventually, "the one who brings the move of God to bear against the enemy."[8]

Eckhardt, pastor and overseer of Crusaders Ministries in Chicago, agrees with Kelly when he notes: "Apostolic ministry is a ministry of warfare. It entails commanding, mobilizing, rallying and gathering the army of God to challenge and pull down the strongholds of the enemy." Therefore, an apostolic leader "invades new territories and breaks through. The apostolic leader has the ability to go first. He or she is the first to encounter the spiritual resistance of the powers of darkness and the first to penetrate the barriers they erect."[9]

Apostle as Spiritual Father Figure

Besides an apostle being a warrior-apostle, Kelly also portrays an apostle as a father who will prepare his sons and daughters for future warfare. He states: "our success should be measured by the quality of the sons and daughters whom we are preparing."[10] Wagner puts the role of the apostle as:

> Warfare is the number-one role of the apostle. Prophets will woo you with the Word of the Lord; teachers will educate you; pastors will help you through your problems and hurts; evangelists will get folks saved; but it is the apostle who will declare war on the enemy and lead the church to war. The apostle is the one who will unify

---

7. Kelly, *End Time Warriors*, 54.
8. Kelly, *End Time Warriors*, 54.
9. Kelly, *End Time Warriors*, 64.
10. Kelly, *End Time Warriors*, 13.

the church into a fighting force. The apostle is the one who will bring all past and present truth and every past and present move of God to bear against the enemy.[11]

Having stated the fact that an Apostle is a father who "will prepare his sons and daughters for future warfare," the Apostolic Movement stresses another aspect of being a leader within churches: that of being a warrior.

David Cannistraci also insists that "the apostle will take on the mantle of a father in this coming movement."[12] According to his argument, when God restores the fathers to the body of Christ, the leadership structure automatically shifts its dynamic.[13] It is not an authoritarian leadership structure to him, but the father-son relationship which is mirrored in the spiritual father-son interaction within the kingdom.

Apostle as a Pastor in the Local Church

Dick Iverson, chairman of Ministers Fellowship International, states, "An apostle is a voice unto the churches; one who comes alongside local elders to strengthen and adjust, but not to take dominion over the churches."[14] Wagner mentions that in 2 Corinthians 1:24, it states: "We do not have dominion over your faith but are helpers (partners) of your joy."[15] I conclude then that, for Iverson, apostolic ministry basically means, "pastoring pastors," whereas, for Wagner, the ministry of apostle is the relational covering and network for like-minded church leaders.

The apostolic leadership team includes apostles and elders of the church who oversee the whole fellowship as a team. "Elders are the parents of the church, Iverson says."[16] They are committed to minister to the fellowship and "to avoid any kind of controlling hierarchy."[17] The positive elements that bring a fellowship together are strong relationships with each other, maintaining utmost integrity, and keeping the same doctrinal compatibility.

11. Wagner, *New Apostolic Reformation Church*, 54.
12. Cannistraci, *Apostles*, 118.
13. Cannistraci, *Apostles*, 118–28.
14. Wagner, *New Apostolic Reformation Church*, 171.
15. Wagner, *New Apostolic Reformation Church*, 174.
16. Wagner, *New Apostolic Reformation Church*, 173.
17. Wagner, *New Apostolic Reformation Church*, 176.

Apostle as Pioneer

Roberts Liardon, president of Roberts Liardon Ministries, states: "An apostle is one who builds ministry from nothing."[18] In other words, an apostle is one who "works for pioneering work and who builds the ministry from scratch. The apostolic ministry is not so much to network the present ministries, but rather to pioneer and send people to the nations."[19] One significant paradigm for Liardon's ministry is that they see church growth as how many people they are sending out rather than how many people are in the church. In other words, church growth is not dependent on the number of local members but rather on the releasing of the saints to the nations in order to fulfill the Great Commission. "Go" is the catch phrase for Liardon's ministry.

Liardon stresses the word "first" in 1 Corinthians 12:28: "God hath set some in the church, first as apostles." The Greek word *proton*, "first," means "first in time order or rank."[20] The role for apostle is, thus, being a pioneer and going into a territory first.

Apostle as Church Planter

Pastor Larry Kreider, DOVE Christian Fellowship International, writes: "Those involved in the true apostolic movement of this century love the Lord fervently, love his body passionately, and are committed to helping fulfill the Great Commission."[21] He continues:

> Unlike an association of churches that gives ordination and general accountability to church leaders, we see an apostolic movement as a family of churches having a common focus: a mandate from God to labor together to plant and establish churches throughout the world.[22]

For him, apostolic ministry is to mobilize and empower God's people to fulfill his purposes. Every DOVE cell group has a vision to plant new cells as well as partnering the work of church planting throughout the world.

---

18. Liardon, "Embassy Christian Center," 117.
19. Liardon, phone interview with the author, September 2005.
20. Liardon, "Embassy Christian Center," 49.
21. Kreider, "Dove Christian Fellowship International," 103.
22. Kreider, "Dove Christian Fellowship International," 107.

A crucial aspect of cell group ministry is to train future spiritual parents so that they may give themselves to their spiritual children—being a family as they demonstrate their love to one another. It took time for Kreider to transition to the "give the church away" vision. He recognized that the Lord called him to be part of an apostolic movement by "building a relationship with Jesus, with one another, and to reach the world from house to house, city to city, and nation to nation."[23]

It is worth noting that none of the New Apostolic leaders acknowledge the prophets, evangelists, and teachers as gifts with whom they need to colabor together. I will critique the practice of New Apostolic leadership in the light of biblical inspiration on apostleship in Part II.

Defining the Apostle-Concept as Used by the NARC Leaders

In this section, I summarize the emails and the interviews conducted with the New Apostolic leaders. The selection of these particular New Apostolic leaders is based on those Wagner quotes and affirms. It is also based on the characteristics of what Wagner considers key roles of these leaders in the NARC. This set of characteristics will enable me to critique the NARC in chapters 5, 6, and 7.

Apostleship as a Gift to the Individual

The development of apostleship is largely characterized by a shift in understanding of the "apostle" first as a gift to the individual, then later as an office or title within the church. Wagner states: "Apostle is a spiritual gift."[24] He provides a working definition as follows:

> The gift of apostle is the special ability that God gives to certain members of the body of Christ to assume and exercise general leadership over a number of churches with an extraordinary authority in spiritual matters that is spontaneously recognized and appreciated by those churches.[25]

---

23. Kreider, "Dove Christian Fellowship International," 106.
24. Wagner, *Churchquake,* 104.
25. Wagner, *Churchquake,* 105.

Wagner goes on to say that this definition applies to "the majority of apostles, but not to all," and states that he will defer the identification of the various kinds of apostles to a future date.

Apostleship as the First Rank

Wagner contends: "Conversely, the principal characteristic that distinguishes apostles from other members of the body of Christ is individual authority."[26] To him, the extraordinary authority of an Apostle is the most distinguishable characteristic.[27] Quoting from 1 Corinthians 12:28, Wagner insists that God delegated greater authority to an apostle. Based on his interpretation of 1 Corinthians 12:28, "first" implies a divine ordering[28] and means that God specially exalted an apostle as the first rank of all other gifts.[29]

In agreeing with Wagner, Eckhardt goes further to explain the word "first" in 1 Corinthians 12:28. His main point is that an apostle is first and foremost sent by the risen Lord. Therefore, the apostolic anointing is the dominant anointing of the church. This is the foundational argument of Eckhardt, which comes from his understanding of the apostolic commission. He believes that the commission Jesus gave the church can be defined as an apostolic commission. Because of the apostolic commission, an apostolic anointing must to be the foundational anointing of the church.[30]

---

26. Wagner, *Changing Church*, 31.
27. Wagner, *Changing Church*, 165.
28. Wagner, *Changing Church*, 167.
29. Wagner, *Changing Church*, 168.
30. Eckhardt, *Leadershift*, 11–12.

Table 3

Critique of the Definition of Apostleship in NARC

	Term	Author	Meaning	Bible reference
Definition	**Apostle**	**From**	**Origin of apostle-viewpoint**	
In Secular Greek	Apostolos	Agnew	1. Messenger and sent	
	Apostello	D. Muller	2. Sending of persons with a commission 3. A divine sending and authorization	
	Apostolos	Kruse	4. Authorized agent 5. having been sent	
In OT and Rabbinic Judaism	Saliah	Lightfoot Rengstorf Kirk	6. Sent man 7. Commissioned agent 8. One sent to act in the name of another ambassador	John 13:16 2 Cor 8:23 Phil 2:25
In Gnosticism	Apostolate	Schmithals	9. Appropriation of the missionary office of Jewish	
Definition	**of Apostle**	**By**	**NT**	
	Twelve	Agnew Kirk Brown Hahn Betz	10. one who, through a vision of the risen Lord 11. Has become an official witness to this resurrection 12. Who has been commissioned by him to preach the gospel in a way fundamental to its spread	2 Cor 1:1 Luke 6:13–16 Matt.10:1–4 Mark 3:14–19 Acts 1:13f Gal 1:1 Rom 1:1 1 Cor 15:9
	Apostolic men	Ferguson	13. Missionary 14. Apostolic men who are associates of the Twelve and Paul	Luke 10:1
	Apostolos	Plummer	15. A messenger 16. Accredited representative, envoy 17. Missionary who fulfilling the gospel	2 Cor 8:23 Phil 2:25 Rom 1:1 Eph 3:2–7 1 Tim 2:7

Eckhardt goes on to emphasize "apostle" as a gift and stresses: "apostles are first in rank" and "apostolic ministry operates at a rank high enough to speak on behalf of heaven." He states that even though all Christians are equal in Christ, "there are different ranks in the Spirit."[31] He indicates that apostolic authority carries more authority and power than any other authority within the body of Christ. He quotes 1 Corinthians 12:28 as a biblical basis for his argument. He states: "rank is a degree or position of dignity, eminence, or excellence; a grade of official standing."[32] For Eckhardt, while "apostle" is defined as a gift, the "apostle" as a position or office starts to emerge in his thoughts as shown above in a hierarchical fashion.

A key word to define the role of apostle is "authority" for both Wagner and Eckhardt.[33] Therefore, they view the authority of apostle through the grid of authority which places high stress on the rank or the order of an apostle within the structure of the movement.[34]

Critique of the NARC Based on a Biblical Framework for Apostle

In this section, with the biblical framework for apostle from chapters 1 and 2, I will compare and contrast the definition of apostleship in the NT and the definition of Apostleship in the NARC.

The biblical definition of apostle strongly emphasizes the aspect of being a "sent one." The sharpest contrast between NARC's apostleship and the biblical definition of apostleship is this focus on the primary definition of apostle. The world *apostolos* stresses the "sent" part of apostleship rather than leadership over local churches. While the NARC emphasizes apostleship as the highest gift among all other gifts, they lose the focus of "sent one" as the primary definition of apostleship.

A second contrast is the connotation of an apostle as title between the NARC and the biblical definition of apostleship. Within NARC circles, it is a norm to use Apostle as the title of apostolic leadership which then leads to focus on spiritual authority rather than the primary biblical function of the one who is "sent."

---

31. Eckhardt, *Moving in the Apostolic*, 45.
32. Eckhardt, *Moving in the Apostolic*, 45.
33. Eckhardt, *Moving in the Apostolic*, 105.
34. Eckhardt, *Moving in the Apostolic*, 105.

Comparison on the Role of Apostleship

In this section, I critique the role of apostleship as understood in the NT and the NARC. Table 4 is a partial selection from the previous chapter.

Critique of Apostle as Pastor in the Local Church

The role of apostleship in the NT strongly relies upon the role of Christ's apostles in pioneering and planting churches in the first-century world. The NT limits the role of apostolic gifting to planting churches and carrying out Jesus' commission before he ascended to heaven. Strictly speaking, there is no indication of the role of apostle as the pastoral leader over the local church in the NT.[35]

To confirm the critique of apostolic leadership being part of the leadership of the church, Martin Garner provides a succinct theological statement of understanding the gift and the role of apostle in his book.[36] According to Garner, the definition of "a sent one" as an apostle means "pioneering, breaking ground, and going with nothing," rather than functioning in a pastoral role in the local church.

---

35. Wagner, *Churchquake*, 107.
36. Garner, *Call for Apostles Today*, 10–13.

Table 4

Critique of the Role of Apostleship in NARC

Role of	Apostle	By	NT	
	Twelve	Betz	18. By their testimony and work of planting churches, they formed the foundation of the church	Acts 1:21–26 Eph 2:20 Rev 21:14 Matt 10:1–2 Mark 3:14 Mark 6:30
Book of Matthew	Apostle	Kruse	19. Carrying on the Great Commission	Matt 28:18–20
Book of Mark	Apostle	Green	20. Preach the good news to all creation	Mark 16:15–16
Book of Luke	Apostle	Green	21. Witnesses to the death and resurrection of Jesus Christ, to call for repentance, and offer forgiveness in his name	
Book of John	Apostle	Green	22. Doing an extension of Jesus' ministry	John 20:21
	Apostle	Betz	23. Founding churches	Phil 1:1, 2:25
	Apostle	Kirk	24. Church planter 25. Build-up the church	Eph 4:11–16 1 Cor 14:1–26
Eph 4:11–13 and 1 Cor 12:28	Apostle	Talbert Fee	26. One who has a ministry that comes first, chronologically, for pioneering churches	1 Cor 12:28
		Collins	27. One who lays a foundation for the church	1 Cor 12:28

A Critique of the Apostle Concept in NARC

In order to gain assistance in my comparison of the NT with the NARC and then the critique of apostolic concept, I present Table 5 which complements Table 1.

Table 5
Critique of the Concept of Apostleship in NARC

Concept of	Apostle	By	NT	
	Apostle	Betz	28. Not appointed by human authorities, but by the risen Christ himself, either personally or by revelation 29. Witnessing the resurrection	1 Thess 2:7 Col 1:24 2 Cor 5:16 1 Cor 15:10 Gal 1:1,12,15–16 1 Cor 1–5
	Apostellein	Hahn	30. Prophetic vocation	
	Apostolos	Plummer	31. One who performs "signs, wonders and miracles" only for the divine confirmation of the gospel	2 Tim 1:10–11
Eph 4:11–13 and 1 Cor 12:28	Apostle	Talbert Fee Collins	32. A spiritual gift for the church (Apostle-concept) 33. A tool to equip the church (Apostle-concept)	Eph 4:11–13 1 Cor 12:28
	Jesus as Apostle		34. Incarnational-humble servant	

Critique of Apostleship as the First Rank

In the NT, the phrase "first of all" from 1 Corinthians 2:28 is understood as the role of apostle (see numbers 26 and 27 from Table 4), however, NARC's understanding of "first of all" led the apostle to be the first hierarchical rank of the leadership as well as the first hierarchical rank of all other gifts.

According to Wagner, an apostle is a leader in the church who is "specially anointed, with greater authority, and exalted by God."[37][38] To him, the evidence of the gift of apostle can often be manifested in signs, wonders, and miracles. This means that spiritual authority will be recognized by spiritual gifts. Consequently, the question in terms of leadership structure is how hierarchical can that be, how much power does an apostle exercise

---

37. Wagner, *Changing Church*, 165.
38. Wagner, *Churchquake*, 105.

based on that spiritual authority, and to whom is the apostle accountable in terms of spiritual authority? The assumption of spiritual authority within the NARC creates conflict between their own belief system and practice. According to Ephesians 4:11–13, the main point is to train and equip saints to do good works. However, this understanding of an apostle's spiritual authority leaves the rest of the believers as passive followers. Gibbs points out the downfall of recognizing the authority by apostolic anointing that many "dare not question any of his decisions for fear of incurring divine displeasure for opposing or even questioning 'the Lord's anointed.'"[39]

A Critique of Apostleship as Gift to the Individual

In the NT, the gift of apostle is understood as being to equip the saints; thus, the gift of apostle is given to the church. On the contrary, among the NARC, the gift of apostle is given to the individual.[40] This means that the gift of apostle creates position and title, rather than the work of apostolic gifts. The phrase "first of all" from 1 Corinthians 12:28 should be interpreted for the primary role of apostle first in a chronological sense, rather than the NARC interpretation of "first of all" as the first rank of all other gifts. The NARC leadership sees the gift of apostle as the highest quality among all the other gifts. As a result in the NARC, it is common to find the gift of apostle placed at the top over all other leadership.[41]

Eckhardt states that even though all Christians are equal in Christ, "there are different ranks in the Spirit."[42] He indicates that apostolic authority carries more authority and power than any other authority within the body of Christ. He quotes 1 Corinthians 12:28 as a biblical background of his argument. He defines, "rank is a degree or position of dignity, eminence, or excellence; a grade of official standing."[43]

This approach brings serious contrast between the biblical understanding of apostolic leadership and NARC's understanding of the gift of apostle. It appears to be a Holy Spirit-centered vision, based on the movement or workings of the Holy Spirit; but in reality, the leadership or church structure basically inherited the modern church legacy. And when that

39. Gibbs, *Church NEXT*, 75.
40. Wagner, *Churchquake*, 104.
41. Eckhardt, *Moving in the Apostolic*, 45.
42. Eckhardt, *Moving in the Apostolic*, 45.
43. Eckhardt, *Moving in the Apostolic*, 45.

institutional, hierarchical legacy was baptized with the "power of the Holy Spirit" as manifested through the central figures of this new Holy Spirit movement, an apostle-centric leadership was born, in which the authority is further concentrated and consolidated into the "Apostle." This resulted in a tendency to nullify the system of accountability that previously existed in church structures. Consequently, as will become evident in my case studies in Part II of this book, it is difficult for the NARC to avoid becoming a "hierarchical organization" where much focus and honor is placed on a high-ranking Apostle.[44]

To confirm Hans Kung's understanding of *charisma* as gracious, not controlling, Gibbs brings a sharp contrast between the controllers and those who empower in terms of how to release people in order for them to use their "God-given gifts in response to a God-given calling."[45] He states: "Controllers deprive others of the opportunity to grow and mature through learning, through having their faith stretched as they reach for the unlikely and the seemingly impossible."[46] The crucial point, he goes on to say, is that churches must live out the biblical apostolic paradigm. The apostolic paradigm will define the church's "risk-taking initiatives" and "willingness" in terms of casting the apostolic vision to venture into new territory.[47]

Reflection

On the whole, with these limitations acknowledged, it is worth noting that "clearly contemporary claimants to the office of an Apostle cannot be regarded as equivalent to the first-century apostles of Christ."[48] Gibbs differs from the NARC's interpretation that the office of apostle will be "restored and authenticated by the same miraculous gifts and authority over churches."[49] Gibbs points out the non-biblical perspective on this position in terms of their miracle-working credentials, effectiveness in church planting, and the process of appointing the title of apostle.[50] The NARC, therefore, must be critiqued in light of the biblical perspective. It is impor-

---

44. Wagner, *Churchquake*, 105.
45. Gibbs, *Church NEXT*, 70–71.
46. Gibbs, *Church NEXT*, 70.
47. Gibbs, *Church NEXT*, 233–34.
48. Gibbs, *Church NEXT*, 76.
49. Gibbs, *Church NEXT*, 76.
50. Gibbs, *Church NEXT*, 76–77.

tant for the comparison to be derived this way. Only then can the NARC understanding be critiqued, not in terms of their own standards, but by virtue of God's expectations.

The NARC Development of Apostolic Church Concepts

From the above argument, understanding what an apostle is and what the apostolic foundational government should look like within the NARC is by no means simple. The description of the apostolic foundational government stops with the promotion of it. It fails to explain in detail how the apostolic movement with its five-fold ministry and officers should be established, and how that five-fold ministry and officers ought to function to equip the saints with the five-fold gifts.

In this section, I give an overview of the New Apostolic Ministry through a literature review, similar to the overview I presented in chapter 2 with respect to the meaning of apostleship.

Five-Fold Ministry

The key concept to understanding the Apostolic Church ministry among the NARC depends on an awareness of the five-fold ministry based on Ephesians 4:11–13. This provided the rationale for my presentation of an exegesis of this passage in chapter 2. According to Eckhardt, the main purpose of God in raising an apostolic leader is to release believers. He puts the goal of the apostolic anointing on equipping and releasing believers.[51] Even though the NARC believes that the five-fold ministry is the authentic apostolic ministry, the reality is to emphasize the apostolic anointing rather than equipping saints along with the other four gifts in Ephesians 4:11–13. I look closely at this issue in the following chapters.

The biblical understanding of the church's ministry can be summed up by reflecting upon Jesus' ministry, in which He proclaims the Kingdom of God through preaching and healing. The biblical ecclesiology reflects God's attributes as a way of participating in his mission in the world. When the church begins to make disciples, the faith community begins to emerge. The faith community is not just for existing, but also for witnessing God's attributes and the gospel to the unchristian community. Because biblical

---

51. Eckhardt, *Leadershift*, 28.

ecclesiology focuses on the ministry of Jesus, Paul argued that there is no need to have hierarchical order to form the faith community. To Paul, the biblical church is an organic family which exercises gifts to each other as a loving family. Echoing Paul's design of the church, Snyder critiques the hierarchical concept of church's structure.[52] If that is true, then the main purpose for the five-fold gifts in Ephesians 4:11–13 is to complete equipping the saints for the work of proclaiming, teaching, and healing, as Lincoln insists[53]

The main pitfall of the NARC's understanding of the church is its loss of focus on God's intention for the gifts. The NARC made a mistake in over-exalting the gift of apostle, against God's primary intention. For instance, when Cannistraci highlights the apostle's work in terms of bringing maturity to the body of Christ, he argues:

> Paul clearly says that apostles will function until the body of Christ is fully matured. Others have maintained that even if apostles do exist, they are expected to bear the weight of all apostolic work. Let the apostles do the apostolic work.[54]

In addition to Cannistraci, Eckhardt also explains how an apostolic anointing is key to fulfill the Great Commission. He states: "The church for years has been taught that the Great Commission is an evangelistic commission." However, he feels it is also an apostolic commission. "The commission was given to apostles, and it will take an apostolic anointing and strategy to fulfill it."[55] He also missed the point that the biblical concept of Missional Church neither depends on the five-fold ministry nor on the apostle's work only. Rather, the biblical concept of Missional Church values the ministry of Jesus over the anointing of an apostle.

Defining Second Reformation Restorative Ministry

Wagner defines the "New Apostolic Reformation" as "an extraordinary work of God at the close of the twentieth century that is, to a significant extent, changing the shape of Protestant Christianity around the world."[56]

---

52. Snyder and Runyon, *Decoding the Church*, 108–9.
53. Lincoln, *Ephesians*, 254.
54. Cannistraci, *Apostles*, 51.
55. Eckhardt, *Leadershift*, 57.
56. Wagner, *New Apostolic Reformation Church*, 19.

Wagner was echoing Donald Miller's statement in terms of using the word "reformation" when he stated: "I believe we are witnessing a second reformation that is transforming the way Christianity will be experienced in the new millennium." He also believes that as the sixteenth century was the first Protestant reformation, since then, we are experiencing "the most radical change in world Christianity."[57]

He distinguished, however, between the reformation of the sixteenth century and the current one, observing the fact that the current reformation focuses more on a practice rather than faith.

Furthermore, he provides alternate names for the NARC churches: Post-denominational churches, independent churches, charismatic churches, restoration churches, grassroots churches, neo-denominational churches, new-paradigm churches, and the next church. It is worth noting, that he saw something different enough in the "nature of the New Apostolic Reformation" and felt it warranted a new name that reflected the ideas in such a list. Included in his rationale for choosing NARC instead of using any of these names are the following:

- There are still "denominational churches" within this movement like the Foursquare Church
- 80 percent of the NARC are charismatic and 20 percent are non-charismatic, such as the Crystal Cathedral, Willow Creek Community Church, and Community Church of Joy
- A denomination can be defined as a movement, fellowship, association, network, or family of like-minded, like-faith churches.[58]

Although Miller and Wagner agree with each other in terms of belief that this era is a second reformation, the question that remains is whether the NARC represents "a reconfiguration of existing churchgoers" or "a significant expansion into the unchurched population through effective evangelistic outreach?"[59] Gibbs asserts: "it is still too soon to assess their long-term significance."[60] Wagner once stated: "If the name works, it is used. If not, it is discarded to oblivion."[61] He concludes that only history

---

57. Wagner, *Churchquake,* 36.
58. Wagner, *Churchquake,* 38–42.
59. Gibbs, *Church NEXT,* 18.
60. Gibbs, *Church NEXT,* 18.
61. Wagner, *Churchquake,* 34.

can tell whether things work or not in terms of using the NARC as the name for this movement.

Defining New Ministry Focus

Wagner explains the "Five Compass-point NARC Values" as follows:

- Theology has absolute norms
- Ecclesiology looks outward
- Eschatology is optimistic
- Organization emerges from personal relationships
- Leaders can be trusted.[62]

Wagner also made an interesting observation between the values of the NARC and the transition from modern to post-modern culture:

- From position-based to vision- and values-based
- From rigid to flexible
- From passion for order to tolerance of ambiguity
- From control to coordination
- From why to why not?
- From boundary making to boundary breaking
- From permission withholding to empowerment.[63]

Wagner sees many parallel trends between a cultural transition and a church transition.[64] Essentially, the value of the organization of the NARC ministry can be illustrated as a transition from organization-prioritized to relational, organic, people-prioritized.

Having identified some of the characteristics, it is important to take a look at whether these values are actually being practiced and explored within the NARC. According to Wagner, the NARC refrains from being "positional-based, rigid, controlling, boundary making, [and] permission

---

62. Wagner, *Churchquake*, 64–78.
63. Wagner, *Churchquake*, 73.
64. Wagner, *Churchquake*, 73.

withholding," but, rather, to be "flexible, coordinating, breaking boundaries, and empowering."[65]

Defining New Outreach

The rise of apostolic ministry is, according to Breen, "a sovereign work of God."[66] He continues: "God is allowing the decline of mainstream Christianity to follow the social and cultural changes in the West, while at the same time bringing about a new church movement committed to an apostolic mission."[67] The decline of established Christianity in the West is characterized by its failure to reach out to and to save the lost. Breen points to the contemporary church's failure to evangelize, and, likewise, envisions a shift:

> From being evangelical churches to becoming evangelizing churches, from evangelism as a hiccup in the life of the church to evangelism as the heartbeat in the life of the church . . . The style of evangelism in a post-modern environment is very different from that in a modern environment.[68]

This emphasis on evangelism is central to the NARC, though more in depth analysis into the movement reveals how it is distinct from the Missional Church movement.[69]

Breen strongly believes that the "end time" harvest requires "end-time Apostles." He adds that, "we are facing for the first time in human history the possibility of reaching every people group on earth (there are fewer than 500 unreached people groups calculated) is within our grasp in the next few years."[70] He insists that Apostles are the ones who are providing the direction and definition of the task of the end time ministries.[71] Thus, the restoration of the apostles from the early church is crucial to the task at hand.[72]

---

65. Wagner, *Churchquake*, 73.
66. Breen, *Apostle's Notebook*, 17.
67. Breen, *Apostle's Notebook*, 27.
68. Breen, *Apostle's Notebook*, 30.
69. See chapter 10.
70. Breen, *Apostle's Notebook*, 18.
71. Breen, *Apostle's Notebook*, 19.
72. Breen, *Apostle's Notebook*, 20.

Defining New Ecclesiology

A significant number of new apostles have risen since 1990 in North America within the Apostolic Churches. Both Eckhardt and Wagner are well known apostles in the New Apostolic Movement. Eckhardt has been a forerunner apostle in his church since 1990. He contends that this New Apostolic Movement is God's plan to lead his church to the final victory.[73] Relating to the leadership shift in the twenty-first century, Eckhardt identifies the apostle at the center of the moveable leadership within the Body of Christ.[74] The function of the apostle is mainly to impart gifts within the Body of Christ, thereby enhancing growth within the church.

Thus, the NARC is a counterforce to modern Ecclesiology. Ephesians 4:11–13 has been the NARC's key verse, stressing the need to equip the saints for the work of ministry. Therefore, in an individual NARC, the main job of a senior pastor, the Apostle, is to equip the congregation to do the ministry. Instead of pastoral counseling, visiting the sick, and so forth, this is what the modern church understands is part of the senior pastor's job description. The NARC organizes programs for evangelism, social services, and community activities; however, they do not form a church bureaucracy like modern churches often do, but see these activities as ways in which they can serve the community's needs.

Contrary to the model of modern churches, the New Apostolic ministry does not exist in order to preserve or maintain the institution itself; but rather, it functions around a structured and linear form of ministry in order to be effective in service. Despite the attempt to avoid church bureaucracy, the structure of the NARC remains hierarchical.

NARCs come out of counter-cultural, not so much emerging soil. The word "restoration" is often employed by apostolic leaders to describe the biblical background of this movement, indicating that the modern church is in need of fixing. The NARC movement was born out of holy frustration with the current state of churches, where the church failed to be the church and had no power. In short, Apostolic Churches restored things that became absent in denominational churches in the 1980s and onward.

---

73. Eckhardt, *Moving in the Apostolic*, 17–18.
74. Eckhardt, *Leadershift*, 1–12.

Defining New Authority Structure

Wagner states that apostolic leadership within the NARC is transitioning "from bureaucratic authority to personal authority, from legal structure to relational structure, from control to coordination, and from rational leadership to charismatic leadership."[75] The relational authority structure tends to be recognized by a spiritual anointing, as Gibbs points out.[76] Reflecting on what Kung writes, a true charisma can be described as love, service, and call.[77] He insists that the mark of a charismatic leader is serving people with an extraordinary and wonderful gift of grace.[78] It is important to remember that a biblical authority is marked by neither signs nor wonders, miracles nor anointing, but is marked by love for others, genuine service for others, and obedience to one's calling.

Defining New Financing Concept

The NARC believes that if they give to the church, it will be given to them even in greater measure (Luke 6:38). Compared to other denominational churches, the tithes and offerings are expected in a generous way. They learn and believe that giving is beneficial and cheerful. It is evident that the focus of teaching on financial prosperity is often related to the mindset of giving. Because of this belief, the NARC faces few financial problems. They believe that this is a new financial situation with which NARC is blessed.

Define New Worship Style

The role of worship within the NARC is derived from an appreciation of the Holy Spirit in the context of contemporary culture.[79] Wagner states that the eight most significant changes within the NARC are: contextual participation, songs not hymns, percussion not pipe organs, celebration, focusing on intimacy with God, liberty, and missions.[80]

---

75. Wagner, *New Apostolic Reformation Church*, 20.
76. Gibbs, *Church NEXT*, 75.
77. Kung, *Church and Ecumenism*, 58–59.
78. Kung, *Church and Ecumenism*, 59.
79. Wagner, *Churchquake*, 153.
80. Wagner, *Churchquake*, 157–58.

People in the NARC worship with body language, applause, and flow.[81] The worship leaders strive to be sensitive to the Holy Spirit as they lead the congregation to minister to the Lord and get in touch with God. Wagner uses Ron Kenoly, worship leader of a NARC in San Jose, to define the function of a worship leader:

> The function of a worship leader is to bring other people into God's presence. I'm often asked how I know when I have accomplished my job. The truth is that it's not something I see with the natural eye. I do not have a written formula. Sometimes I know I'm finished when I can feel the presence of the Lord in the room so strong that I know the only thing left for me to do is to get out of God's way. Many times it is not appropriate for me to say or do anything.[82]

Gibbs quotes comments from the traditional denominational leaders in regards to receiving challenges and inspirations by NARC churches. He says: "they demonstrate renewed spiritual vitality and a commitment to the mission, resulting in transformed lives, numerically growing churches, and the planting of new churches."[83] He also provides the twelve empirical indicators of a Missional Church.[84] The point is that a Missional Church understands God's mission calls and sends the church to be a missionary in society and in the culture.[85]

Eckhardt adds by emphasizing: "Go into all the world and preach the gospel to every creature, and make disciples of all the nations is a commission for the church."[86] It is missional and it is apostolic. Wagner insists: "Apostolic Churches, by nature, give high priority to reaching out effectively to the unchurched."[87]

Reflection

Based on the proponents of the NARC, one can summarize the characteristics of the NARC as follows:

81. Wagner, *Churchquake*, 171.
82. Wagner, *Churchquake*, 174.
83. Gibbs, *Church NEXT*, 18.
84. Gibbs, *Church NEXT*, 52.
85. Gibbs, *Church NEXT*, 51.
86. Eckhardt, *Moving in the Apostolic*, 37, 119.
87. Wagner, *Churchquake*, 45.

- Having a "new" name to distinguish themselves from others
- New authority structure led by "charismatic" pastor-leaders who are seen as apostles with a vision for what people can become
- Strong leadership training and lay ministries
- New ministry focus, small groups, family feeling, but not exclusivity
- New worship style
- New prayer forms and an earnestness in prayer
- New financing
- New outreach, compassion for the lost, many ministries to the unchurched, obedience to the Great Commission, cultural adaptation to the target population
- New power priorities, and passion for outpouring of God's Spirit.[88]

These nine characteristics have a main role in my analysis of the data from the three case studies in Part II. Now I bring critique of the Apostolic Church concept in the NARC based on the critique-framework for missional ecclesiology.

Critique of Apostolic Ministry that is Missional

The purpose of critiquing apostolic ministry within NARC is to define and clarify the biblical meaning of church ministry, and then bring realization of the reason why an apostle is necessary in the ministry of the NARC. The biblical purpose of church ministry is to bring Jesus' mission to the world as a faith community.

In terms of understanding apostolic leadership, the literature review of Wagner's writings defines apostolic leadership manifested in the area of spiritual authority and leadership structures, and especially the spiritual authority of an apostle who serves as the founding pastor of such a church. His emphasis is not on "missional sending," but more on the function of an apostle within the leadership structure of a church. In other words, the meaning of apostolic leadership is portrayed not as a "sent one," but "the leadership of the church." This, indeed, suggests that the Apostolic Church is not very missional, contrary to my understanding of the biblical text, which insists it should be so.

88. Wagner, *New Apostolic Reformation Church*, 18–25.

Critique on Pioneering or Networking

The biblical term for church planting can be identified with pioneering expansion. The Apostolic Church sends apostles to expand territories. Thus, a biblical mission is not to bring an expansion through "reconfiguration among churchgoers," but to bring the unchurched people to the kingdom of God. Gibbs suggests it to be "an open question whether they represent a reconfiguration of existing churchgoers or a significant expansion into the unchurched population through effective evangelistic outreach."[89]

The question is, therefore, whether the expansion of the NARC is coming from the unchurched population or a reconfiguration of existing churchgoers? I will continue this critique when I analyze the three NARC case studies. Through the NARC case studies, the distinction between pioneering and networking will be revealed and critiqued as well.

Critique on the Apostle Alone or Five-Fold Ministry

The development of an understanding of what makes an apostle, and what the apostolic foundational government should look like, stops with promotion of the apostolic foundational government, in which there is a five-fold ministry with five-fold offices. How the five-fold ministry ought to function to equip the saints has not been explicated. This would explain the failure to execute the perspective that has been put forth by Wagner.

The biblical meaning of apostolic ministry embraces the five-fold ministry. Apostolic ministry recognizes a form of hierarchy, but not in a dictatorial form. We must not imagine that one person in the body of Christ, however powerful or effective in ministry, can assume the kind of authority that Christ exercised in terms of accountability. Even his twelve were sent out in pairs as a recognition of the inherent incompleteness of one person, regardless of the level of power, gifts, and authority (Luke 10: 1–10). Both Christ and Paul recognized that the ultimate leader of a church is Christ and the church leadership is made up of people with different gifts, who together make up a more complete leadership as each brings his or her gifts to the table.

This means that, while recognizing a place for a top leader or an *apostole*, the top leader must function with accountability and mutual submission to other leaders or offices (prophet, pastor, teacher, and evangelist).

---

89. Gibbs, *Church NEXT*, 18.

Thus, an apostolic leadership is functional (job description) and does not reflect some kind of ontological, positional, or functional superiority. Ontologically speaking, one could argue that the five-fold ministry is equal in importance. If one is exalted above the other, it is an invitation to corruption of gifts and power.

On the whole, the apostolic leaders function in accountability to, partnership with, and mutually submit to other offices or gifts. Each gift or office functions uniquely and equally contributes to the whole of leadership. And each sharpens and shapes the other, so there is a complete cross-fertilization of the offices and gifts.

Summary

The limitations in the implementation of the New Apostolic Ministry can be described in the following three points: first, the definition of "apostle" went through developmental stages, and this opened doors for different levels of implementation by various leaders, either according to one's theological understanding of the relevant biblical texts or according to one's exposure or preference in circumstances.

Second, there is not enough clarity provided by the theorists within NARC on what an apostle is and what the apostolic foundational government should look like. The description of the apostolic foundational government stops with the promotion of it. It fails to explain in detail how the apostolic movement with its five-fold ministry and officers should be established and how that five-fold ministry and officers ought to function in order that the saints may be equipped with the five-fold gifts.

Third, the common limitations in the implementation of the NARC lies in the absence of clear directives, and, in all three cases presented in Part II that follows, the apostleship is affirmed and elevated in the near absence of other gifts or offices.

I will now proceed to a descriptive presentation of three churches I studied as a reflection of the NARC. These cases provide further material for study. As I have tried to compare and contrast the intended meaning of biblical texts relating to the concept of apostle in the NT, and used that to critique Wagner and the leadership of the NARC with respect to their understanding of apostles within the movement, so I will use the case studies to further critique the movement.

Part II

Case Studies

In Part II, I examine three NARCs based on the critique presented in chapter 3. I separate the critique into two parts; one is to critique data in the light of biblical inspiration and the second is to identify a gap between ideal and reality.

Michael Fletcher's understanding and implementation of the apostolic gift is the focus of the first case study in chapter 5. But it is limited to the establishment of an apostle, without four other gifts being established. In the second case study in chapter 6, Mel Mullen, utilizes Wagner's 2002 definition of "apostle," but limits its application to the apostle and prophet, which happens to be the same person. In chapter 7, I will present the final case, Rice Broocks's emphasis on the role of apostle in relationship to the planting of churches as a strategic tool to serve evangelism and outreach that suggests Darrell L. Guder's use of the term "missional" for denominational churches.[1]

To conclude the critique of the preceding data, it is important to take note of the common limitations in the implementation of a NARC in the absence of clear directives. In all three cases, the apostleship is affirmed and elevated in the near absence of other gifts or offices. In

1. Guder, *Missional Church*, 1–17.

chapter 8, I will summarize findings that relate to my data which will scrutinize the leadership and ecclesiology of the current NARC. This critical examination process will be followed by suggestions on how to apply the biblical meaning and function of an apostle to the twenty-first-century apostolic leadership and ministry.

Chapter 4

Study Methodology of Selected New Apostolic Reformation Churches

THE ULTIMATE GOAL OF this case study is to critique the biblical theology of the NARC, and to give a more genuine contribution to the biblical emphasis of the NARC from the broader perspective of the body of Christ. I will attempt to draft indicators of NARC through a congregation's life and also to fine tune the NARC's theory from the NARC's actual ministry fields.

In order to explore the gap between theory, which is manifested in the nine characteristics of NARC, and reality, which can be observed in their data, let me confirm both the regular and irregular indicators, commonalities, and non-commonalities of NARC based on Wagner's nine salient characteristics of the New Apostolic Reformation Church:

1. New name
2. New authority structure; led by "charismatic" pastor-leaders; vision for what people can become
3. New leadership training; strong lay ministries; every member and every seeker receives regular pastoral care from a layperson
4. New ministry focus; small groups; family feeling, but not excusive
5. New worship style
6. New prayer forms; earnest in prayer
7. New financing
8. New outreach; compassion for the lost; many ministries to the unchurched; obedience to the Great Commission; cultural adaptation to the target population
9. New power priorities; passion for outpouring of God's Spirit.[1]

---

1. Wagner, *New Apostolic Reformation Church*, 18–25.

In order to explore the gap between the theory of NARC and the reality of NARC, I will also look for new indicators in the congregation's life.

Since the rise of the Apostolic Church in 1990, there has been very little actual research on the principles of the movement itself. As post-modern churches are going through "the greatest change in the way of doing church since the Protestant Reformation,"[2] research that will position this new movement within the body of Christ as a whole, in its structure and its mission as it relates to the contemporary cultural influence, is of critical importance.

This understanding will, first, lead us to be able to critique NARC in the light of biblical inspiration; secondly, to identify a gap between the ideal and reality within the NARC; and, thirdly, to enhance the effectiveness of mission in Apostolic Churches in the twenty-first century. This understanding will enhance the broader effectiveness of being a Missional Church in North America. Furthermore, the biblical framework has a broader missional significance in that it enables me to contribute to the missional objectives for the manifold ministry of Christ and his church.

Data Collection

The data collection for these case studies consists mainly of interviews and review of documents. I have interviewed declared apostles that include Michael Fletcher, Mel Mullen, and Rice Broocks, as well as their teams. The first case study was done with Apostle Michael Fletcher and the Manna Church, in Fayetteville, North Carolina. The second case study comes from Apostle Mel Mullen, at Word of Life Church, in Red Deer, Alberta, Canada, and the third case study is done with Apostle Rice Broocks at Bethel World Outreach Center, in Brentwood, Tennessee.

Step-by-Step Data Analysis

Once the data was collected, I was able to analyze it by transcribing my texts and reading through the entire manuscript. I brought quotations directly from the material to reflect the correlation between Wagner's identified ideal characteristics and to compare the data in light of the Scriptures. In doing this step I also noted new characteristics which went beyond the ideal

---

2. Wagner, *Churchquake*, 5.

and tried to determine which of these were idiosyncratic to the particular church or reflective of the NARC, whether or not they corresponded to the nine ideal characteristics.

This contrast between the ideal and the real provided information on the gap between Wagner's theory of how the NARC should be, and the actual practices of apostles in their church environments. Finally, as Figure 2 illustrates, I compared these three cases with each other to determine how apostolic leadership was both characterized within each community and the contrast between the various apostles and those with whom they worked; the roles and expectations of those who made up an apostolic team.

Transcribing the Interviews

I transcribed the interviews and as I read through the transcribed text, I tried not to interpret it, but rather I used direct quotations from the original scripts. When I selected direct quotations from the original script, I categorized them into four different topics, namely: the definition of apostle, role of apostle, concept of apostle, and ecclesiology of a particular church. After categorizing the original script, I described them in order to demonstrate the direct quotes from the original script and testify to the veracity of the specific subject.

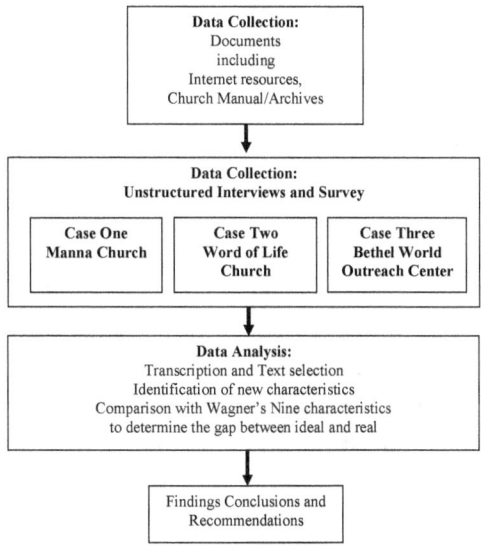

Figure 2
Flow Chart of Data Analysis

Limitation of Data Analysis

The main limitation of data analysis comes from my seven years of ministry exercise within the NARC. I was part of the NARC movement as a full-time staff member. As I noted in the Introduction, my biases may cause my analysis of the data to be completely different from an outsider's view point. However, I have attempted to be as careful as possible to focus on the biblical texts (chapters 2 and 3) and Wagner's criteria for the NARC. Comparison of the case studies with these two primary sets of criteria enabled me to define my findings, leading to specific conclusions about the movement and to make recommendations accordingly.

Data and Documents Collection

In this section, I summarize the documents that I used for this research. There were four different methods that I used during the data collection: documents, archival records, unstructured interview, and participant observation.

The initial data was collected through documents such as administrative documents, web site information, articles from newspapers, and church agenda materials. This data was collected before the actual visit to the site. The interval between data collection and an actual site visit was about six months. Thus, some data from documents did not correspond when the researcher visited the research site. But necessary adjustments were made after the visit. However, the interval between the visit to the research site, and the writing period was about one and a half years. This implies that the quality of the data might be limited because of the interval.

The main data was collected through unstructured interview. The researcher conducted each interview with an unstructured interview questionnaire in written form. Before the actual interview, the interviewee was provided the written form of the unstructured interview questions. Each interview took a minimum of thirty minutes to a maximum of two hours. The unstructured interview was recorded with the permission of the interviewee. The researcher had opportunities to participate in the main worship services, small groups, staff meetings, and the leadership training classes. In terms of validity of my findings, I remain faithful to the original scripts that determine the findings.

Study Methodology

Table 6

Data Collection

	Manna Church Fayetteville, NC	Word of Life Church Red Deer, Canada	Bethel World Outreach Center, TN
Documents: administrative documents, web site, articles from newspaper, agendas, and so on.	• 3 books from senior pastor, Michael Fletcher • "A Vision to Change the World" manual • Welcome package • GCI handbook	• Prayer report from the local news paper • Monthly agendas • Staff meeting agendas	• 1 book from senior pastor, Rice Broocks • Articles from the EN web site • Staff meeting agendas • Training materials
Archival records: service records, organizational records, lists of names, survey data, and so on.	• GCI organizational records • Lists of pastoral and staff members	• Sunday bulletin • 2 teaching CD's of ministry philosophy	• Sunday bulletin • Teaching CD's
Unstructured interview	• 12 pastoral team members [four 90-minute cassette tapes]	• 12 pastoral team members [three 90-minute cassette tapes]	• 17 key pastoral leaders and 3 small group members [five 120-minute cassette tapes]
Participant observation	• Young Adults service	• Regular staff meeting	• Staff meeting • Sunday services • Small group meeting • Leadership training class

Chapter 5

Case Study One: Manna Church

Manna Church is located in Fayetteville, North Carolina. The city of Fayetteville is located next to Fort Bragg and Pope Air Force Base and has a population density of 210,000 people. This city has been named "America's Most Pro-Military Town" by Time Magazine. Apostle Michael Fletcher is the senior pastor of Manna Church, as well as the apostolic team leader of Grace Churches International, a network of 318 churches in over 40 countries worldwide. His main passion is to see other pastors step beyond their current leadership barriers and see their churches become all that God intends for them to be. I was there from April 22–28, 2007, to interview twelve of the pastoral leaders, three cell leaders, and three staff members.

Manna Church Structure

Manna Church has fourteen pastors that include children's pastor, youth pastor, executive pastor, mission pastor, evangelism pastor, and prayer pastor. The leadership team includes the pastors, elders, cell sectional leaders, cell leaders, and two full-time data administrators. The ministries include, among other things, cell groups and campus ministry.

Membership

When new guests arrive, they fill out a card and their information is entered into the data base. If an individual wants to become a member of the church, he or she fills out an application form followed by an interview by people who are trained to present the gospel to them. Afterwards the forms are sent in for data entry. Data entry also includes contributors and contributions. The members are divided by districts, and each district pastor has their own report of the people corresponding to their district. The ethnic make-up of the congregation members include: Caucasian, African-American, Hispanic, and Asian. The church regularly has visitors from all over the world including the Philippines and England. One unique characteristic of the church is its location in a military town. Family members from other countries visit soldiers and then visit the church. Therefore, the ethnic diversity is a major attribute of the church. There are five full-time staff, two part-time staff, and many volunteers serving in campus ministry.

Cell Groups

With a congregation of 4,000 members, it is impossible for fourteen pastors to get in touch with everyone. Therefore, the small groups, also called "cells," are the only way for people to connect. There is an effort to encourage members to lead small groups in their homes or meet for Bible studies. In order to help build relationships, learn about and exercise gifts and talents for the ministry, the small group ideally consists of five to six members. There are 243 cells with about 2,000 members actively involved who meet once a week in small groups.

Definition of Apostleship from Fletcher and Manna Congregation

Based on the transcribed text of the interviews with Michael Fletcher, his leadership team, and members of Manna Church, I now relate the definition, role, and concept of apostleship. According to Fletcher, an apostle is "a person who is gifted by God to equip the church with wisdom."[1] He is a pioneer in the sense that he starts new things such as new churches and new ministries. An apostle is "a pastor to pastors." He is involved in helping pastors with "strategies, discovering their vision, helping pastors discover their vision, motivating, inspiring, and depositing faith in them, so that the pastor's vision can be accomplished." An apostle has more than

1. Fletcher, personal interview with the author, 2007.

one function which includes helping pastors grow, "reach their community, their Jerusalem planting churches and reaching out in missions." Fletcher draws the analogy of the apostles' role with that of a builder, bridesmaid to the church being the bride, coach to the players, and a nurturing mother. According to Fletcher, an apostle is an individual of faith and a humble servant. The following text is from a transcribed interview with Michael Fletcher:

> An apostle is a person who is gifted by God to equip the church with wisdom. An apostle starts new things, particularly new churches, and opens up new areas [of ministry]. An apostle is a pastor to pastors, but not in a passive way. Rather, he leads in terms of strategy, helping pastors discover their vision, motivating, inspiring, and depositing faith in them, so that the pastor's vision can be accomplished. An apostle's role has to do with growth, helping pastors reach their community, their Jerusalem; planting churches and reaching out in missions. Apostles have more than one function.

According to one of the pastoral leaders, an apostle is by definition "one who plants churches." This apostle is also expected to be a senior pastor over a local church and is gifted in teaching and able to lead a pastoral team and the congregation in a biblical way.

When compared to the biblical understanding of apostleship, the interview data does not support the biblical definition of an apostle in the Manna Church. Based on Table 1 the definition of apostle focuses on "sending" and "missionary" aspect, whereas both Fletcher and his congregation portray the understanding of an apostle as a gifted senior pastor over a local church. None of the interview data mentions "sent one," "ambassador," or "missionary" aspect.

When compared to Wagner's definition of apostleship, Fletcher's manifestation of apostleship reflects Wagner's earlier understanding of leadership as being "flexible, coordinating, breaking boundaries, and empowering."[2] Both Wagner and Fletcher defined an apostle as a gifted spiritual leader over a local church. Although Wagner mentions a "sent by God" aspect of an apostle, his focus is "to establish the foundational

---

2. Fletcher, personal interview with the author. See appendix E.

government of the local church,"[3] and "setting things in order for the growth and maturity of the local church."[4]

Definition of the Apostolic Role from Fletcher and Manna Congregation

Fletcher considers the strongest role of apostle to be helping other pastors to grow in the area of faith, evangelistic strategy, and reaching out in missions. He testifies how he implements his apostolic role as one strengthening the faith of other pastors, particularly those in his network called Grace Churches International (GCI). He states:

> I'm constantly speaking faith to other pastors in my network called Grace Churches International (GCI). I tell them that I'm not a talented person. From an A to D speaker, I'm a D. People come up to me and say, "Pastor I'm a C." I reply and encourage them: "I am an average guy and if I can do it [growth, evangelism, mission], you can do it. Larry Stockstill, he's a natural. Rick Warren, a natural. The rest of us aren't so. If I can do it, you can do it." So I feel like my part in the body of Christ today is helping the average pastor believe it. These are average people. They are not great speakers or leaders. In the church we planted, in the last 3 years they doubled their attendance to 460, and they got a new building, and they're projecting growth to continue to 600–700 members in the next couple of years. . . . I constantly work in these areas with them, and many churches are growing and developing in maturity in this field. For these churches, the fruits of it are quite evident.

Fletcher emphasizes that he is just as ordinary as most other pastors. Yet, he encourages pastors, that an average person like himself has helped his church to grow and doubled in attendance in just a few years. So, he encourages pastors by saying that "if I can do it, you can do it." As a result, he is able to see the fruit of it in the growth of many churches unto maturity. In this role of encouragement, he also sees himself as an "apostolic teacher."

For pastoral leaders, Fletcher's role as an apostle consists of casting, communicating, and articulating the vision to the church. Part of the vision is "unique and solid revelation" about the Kingdom of God. As an apostle, Fletcher is able to teach about the Kingdom of God and the "right mindset"

3. Wagner, *Spheres of Authority*, 27.
4. Wagner, *Spheres of Authority*, 27.

for everyday living. He teaches his disciples and leadership team how to become a leader in character and also how to make decisions as a leader. He exemplifies excellent character as the leader.

The interview data from Fletcher and the Manna congregation agree with (18) of Table 1, in terms of forming the foundation of the church. The biblical understanding of apostolic role emphasizes (23) "founding churches" and (27) "one who lays a foundation." The data shows weak agreement with the biblical understanding of the apostolic role. The main focus in the role of apostle, from the data, is in building a strong leadership over the local church rather than being a missionary laying a foundation of a church. From (26) the biblical apostle is one who is the first to go to the front line of pioneering the church. However, Fletcher and the Manna's understanding of the role of apostle is to impart vision in pioneering a church, from behind the front line.

Similarly, the data did not measure up to Wagner's understanding of the apostolic role. The ideal role of apostle, for Wagner, is to be a pioneer who goes into a territory first to found a church.[5] In addition to the pioneering aspect of the apostle, Wagner strongly insists that the role of an apostle is to plant and establish churches throughout the world.[6] The main focus of Wagner's ideal role of apostle is in being the pioneer, planter, and missionary. However, Fletcher's and Manna's understanding of the apostolic role remains in the area of building up a healthy local church and nurturing strong leadership within a local church.

Understanding of Apostolic Concept from Fletcher and Manna Congregation

Through teaching, Fletcher emphasizes the apostolic concept. The main focus of the apostle-concept from Fletcher and Manna congregation can be summed up in three areas: Build up the church, equip the church, and against the "first rank" as an apostle.

---

5. Wagner, *Changing Church*, 73.
6. Wagner, *New Apostolic Reformation Church*, 107.

CASE STUDY ONE: MANNA CHURCH

Build Up the Church

Fletcher felt strongly that unless one is "a builder," in addition to being a preacher, one is not going to build the local church. His story confirms how he understood the apostolic concept as one who builds up the church. He reports that he read a book on small groups titled, *Where Do We Go From Here?* by Ralph Neighbor. Then, he gathered his leaders, church elders, and had a leaders' meeting during which they discussed the material, "argued and wrestled over it." Fletcher's goal was to build up the church by raising up and equipping cell leaders. Therefore, he focused on training cell leaders and preaching these concepts regularly. In the interview he explained how he transitioned the Grace Church from a nominal church structure to an apostolic ministry:

> I began building those concepts [apostolic ministry] into their understanding. Along with those concepts, the cell concepts are the corollary concepts that have to be there, or they won't work. That is if you're a minister and you're more important than I am. I'm called to equip you but you are the gain. I am the bridesmaid but you are the bride. . . . I started with the present leaders—the church elders, sold them on it and when I got them in agreement, I went with the leaders. I took a book titled *Where Do We Go from Here?* by Ralph Neighbor. It's about small groups. I sat down with the leaders, read one chapter and had a leaders meeting. We discussed the material and argued and wrestled over it. I trained them slowly. . . . Once the people could see it and I preached it regularly, it's building. You have to be a builder. If a guy is a preacher and not a builder he's not going to build the local church.

As his story shows, Fletcher implemented an apostolic ministry into his local church. He firmly believes the apostle-concept was designed to build up the church and then to equip the church. He not only equips his own local church, but also helps other local churches to be equipped. His primary function as he sees it within the apostolic network, GCI, is to be a builder.

> I spoke in 2005 at our leadership conference and I gave five messages and one was "Church Growth is God's Idea" and then the "Four Soils." We pointed them in the direction of some resources. That was in November. Then we had four meetings throughout the year where we took those concepts and reinforced them. In the second year we chose one of the four and last year in November we

chose "Building an Outreach Culture." so we did the entire conference only on that. Everyone agreed that over five years we would slowly build this DNA into every level (of leadership) so bring all your leaders, bring all your people. So they brought everybody they could bring. Then in these meetings, we have another one next week, we focus. We are on the following year. It means we focus on outreach. Next year we will talk about the "Kingdom of God" for the entire conference. Then all four meetings will deal with that.

Fletcher's primary function as he sees it within the apostolic network, GCI, is to be a builder. He accomplished this through annual leadership conferences. At these conferences he shares some resources and has four meetings throughout the year during which he reinforces these concepts.

Equip the Church

When Fletcher described the purpose of apostolic ministry, he first mentioned the concept of raising up people. He strongly agrees with the biblical perspective on apostle concept for equipping the church. He once heard Tony Benet stating: "Everything you ever needed to reach your city is already inside your house." After listening to this message over twenty-five times, he finally understood that the apostle's job is "not to do the work but to raise up people (passionate people) to do the work." In that regard, he felt that the pastors "have to believe in people and we don't do that enough." These are the people that are "already inside the house" (of the church). He testifies:

> I discovered as a pastor that every successful relationship has certain things in common, whether it is a marriage, child-bearing relationship, or a business. This is my philosophy of people, and well—I will be honest with you—when I first started I didn't want to care much for people. I loved the church and tolerated the people, but God worked in my heart over the years to say, "Michael Fletcher I died for people. This is about people. I want to raise up people. I traded My son for people. You better focus on people."

Fletcher was honest in sharing that he began the ministry with a wrong attitude of just tolerating people even though he "loved the church." God had to work in his heart to care about people and it took years to accomplish it.

Case Study One: Manna Church

Against Wagner's First Rank as an Apostle

Fletcher's understanding of apostleship strongly disagrees with Wagner's understanding of "apostleship as the first rank." According to Fletcher, Paul took "an opposite approach" to his position as an apostle, as one who is last, one who serves people, and not be a first rank of all others. He felt that there is too much emphasis on apostle as one in authority. He mentioned Jesus' comment on "if you want to be the greatest, become the servant" and how he practices it, for example, by parking his car farthest away in the parking lot so others can park closer. He felt that as a way of being a servant, one should "hold people with an open hand." This compels people to "stay in your hand." But if you hold it tight, people are programmed to hate those who control them."

> We had a big philosophical argument about that on Monday. About whether apostolic authority is positional. God made me an apostle and therefore I have apostolic authority. I contended that Paul took the opposite approach. If you read the other stuff not just "I am Paul the apostle," but he says "I was like a mother." He didn't use the word mother but "I nurtured you" and "I worked with my own hands so that you guys wouldn't be inconvenienced."

According to the pastoral leaders and members, Fletcher has many gifts and talents that include; structure, leadership, organization, training, developing, and preparing people for ministry. In this process, Fletcher invests his life in his people, "grow them, disciple them, send them out, and empower them through the relational model." Their understanding of apostolic concept includes one who is "spiritually high enough" to listen and hear God's voice in making decisions, be prophetic in a sense that they can encourage others with prophetic words, be a church planter, and be a leader who equips and trains the church.

A sharp contrast between the biblical concept of apostleship and that of Fletcher and the Manna congregation can be observed in the understanding of apostleship as a gift. The biblical understanding of apostolic concept is that an apostle is a spiritual gift for the church based on Ephesians 4:11–13. However, from Table 1, Fletcher and the Manna congregation agree with (33) a tool to equip the church; and (34) incarnational humble servant as an apostolic concept. Their concept of apostleship highlights apostolic gift to Fletcher meaning that a spiritual gift is for the individual rather than for the church.

The ideal understanding of apostolic concept from Wagner is to distinguish apostles from other members.[7] Fletcher disagrees and goes on to stress the character of being an apostle in terms of being a humble leader: not controlling but demonstrating God's grace. To Fletcher, Wagner's description of an apostle, who is regarded as the first among Christian leaders,[8] is an important mistake in practicing apostleship. He continues to stress an apostolic concept as not dominating over people, but releasing their ability to lead. In contrast to Fletcher, Eckhardt mentions that an apostle has a high-ranking spiritual responsibility.[9] Wagner also asserts that an apostle has different spiritual ranks that carry different degrees of authority and power.[10]

Ecclesiology in the Manna Church

In this section, I review the factors of church growth and signs of being an apostle based on the interviews with the members of Fletcher's local congregation. The factors of church growth and how to recognize an apostolic leader from the perspective of congregation members will help to clarify the ecclesiology within Manna Church.

Factors of Church Growth

There are three evident factors that the congregation understands as factors of church growth: (1) Kingdom-focused mindset, (2) empowering and releasing people, and (3) understanding calling and destiny.

Kingdom-Focused Mindset

Members of Fletcher's congregation believe that the knowledge and understanding of the Kingdom of God is one of the indicators of church growth. Christians need to have a kingdom perspective in whatever they do. This was demonstrated during their outreach ministry. One of the weekend plans was to go out to the downtown area and give out 6,000 invitations

---

7. Wagner, *Changing Church*, 31.
8. Wagner, *Apostles and Prophets*, 30.
9. Wagner, *Apostles and Prophet*, 30.
10. Wagner, *Churchquake*, 45.

to the church. The target of the invitations were the people "who do not come to church and who have never heard the gospel because nobody has ever invited them." This outreach ministry included follow-up phone calls accompanied by home visits to first time visitors to the church. They went "that extra step" to find out if the invited person is a believer or not. If they are not, then, they share the gospel with these individuals. As one puts it:

> In the evangelical community, there has always been a focus on saving souls, and we have that same focus here, but we see saving souls as being part of glorifying the Kingdom of God. Our focus is to glorify God. When you do that, the other parts fall into place. Your heart has to be going in the right direction. You have to have the right heart for people, to catch souls. I would look for someone who has a Kingdom vision and who is interested in spreading the fame of God. That makes a difference.[11]

Thus, their outreach is all about reaching out to the lost. This requires the right attitude and understanding of the "Kingdom vision." By bringing the lost into the Kingdom of God, they are glorifying God and His kingdom.

Empowering and Releasing People

Manna Church has 243 cell groups that meet during the weekdays throughout the city of Fayetteville. This means that they have 243 people to lead small groups as empowered leaders. The cell is a place of ministry where the congregation can exercise their individual gifts in small group settings. A congregation member described the church as "a cell church." The cell group is where one has an opportunity to exercise his or her spiritual gifts. He emphasized the importance of cell groups as follows:

> Sunday is like a celebration, but during the week the small groups meet, and that's where ministry takes place. We believe in having cell groups as an opportunity for having people to exercise their gifts. Rather than someone giving a prophecy on Sunday in front of the whole church they can give the prophecy in their small group and it's able to be judged. The gifts are developed in a small group where they are most comfortable. We believe that everybody has

---

11. Quotes are from church members interviewed. All interviews were conducted in confidentiality, and the name of interviewees are withheld by mutual agreement. See Appendix C, page 189.

gifting and callings. One of the things we want to do is find out what those gifts are, and encourage and provide opportunities for those with the gifts to exercise those gifts. If it's evangelism, we get them involved with evangelism. If its hospitality, then we get them involved in a place where we can use their gifting.

Thus, the gifts can be discovered as well as developed in the context of small group setting. Also, prophecies can be better judged in a smaller setting as opposed to someone prophesying in front of the whole church. There is a premise that everyone has a calling and spiritual gifting from God. Therefore, there is an effort made to find out what the individual's calling and gifting are and provide opportunities to exercise these gifts.

The Manna Church pastoral team described the process of raising up cell leaders like that of Jesus and his twelve disciples. Jesus did not pick those who were highly educated or those who were established in rank. He went out and found twelve men, discipled them, and eventually sent them out. The empowerment of the disciples came through the "relational model." This was considered by the pastoral team as "a restoration of the biblical model of leadership-development." In this relational model, the cell leaders feel released to make mistakes, and feel empowered to make decisions. They called this kind of environment "grace."

Understanding Calling and Destiny

Manna Church members understand one of their growth factors is discovering the calling on their individual lives as well as the corporate calling on Manna Church. They see destiny as a connected matter between congregational members meaning that their destiny is connected to the person right beside them. One of the pastoral team described the danger of just asking any available person to perform certain functions:

> You need to consider what you are asking them to do and if that is their gifting. Sometimes some people are just put into jobs because they are available and willing, but sometimes people are functioning in a place that they are not supposed to be. I ask, is this your giftedness, is this your calling and is this something you have a heart for? Obviously, those are the best team members.

Case Study One: Manna Church
Signs of Being an Apostle

As opposed to the NARC's ideal signs of recognizing an apostolic leader, which consists of signs, wonders, miracles, and spiritual anointing, Manna Church chooses to recognize leaders based on relationships and character.

Relation-Driven Leader

First, it is a norm for Manna Church that they hire their ministry leaders on a relational basis. Secondly, it is a norm for Manna Church that intimate relationship be developed between leaders and congregational members, to ensure there is a sense of connectivity between pastors and congregational members. There is a genuine caring that goes on between pastors and members. One of the leaders described it as follows:

> Family and your needs, they're ready to take care of it. There is no constant need for re-introductions. People want a sense of mom-and-pop service in a Wal-Mart environment. That's what we seek to provide: that people know that we care. They are better able to receive the message because they know the pastors care. There is no sense of disconnection like, well, this pastor doesn't know where I'm living, and people will tune you out. I think that's part of it. He wants them to feel connected because when people feel that way, there is a sense of being willing to put your shoulders to the plough. Not for the purpose of growing the church, but Michael is Kingdom focused, and that's the vision that God has given him: for this church to be an agent of advancing the Kingdom of God.

There is a small, close-knit atmosphere in spite of the large size congregation. The church and the leaders believe in the apostolic five-fold ministry in Ephesians 4:11. Through the five-fold ministry, the church is being "an agent of advancing the Kingdom of God." By providing a sense of connectedness with leaders, church members have "the chance to rub shoulders with us and get the vision" from the leaders. This leads to a sense of empowerment and sense of ownership of the ministry as well.

Focus on Character

Fletcher's leadership team and congregational members speak highly of character and faithfulness as the first qualification of being a mature

Christian and being a leader as well. One of the congregational members expressed that, "In terms of character and faithfulness, not so much spiritual, we want that—we want a godly leader—what we want to see are faithfulness, diligence, and commitment."

Similarly, one of the leaders described their criteria for raising up leaders among the congregation emphasizing character, faithfulness, and the "Manna DNA" as follows:

> The role of character and DNA in leadership within the apostolic team—it is an issue of who they are [second line of leaders in an apostolic church]. Their character and spirituality are very closely related. The other part is that we grow up leaders, [leadership within an apostolic team] and within the Manna Church, with the Manna DNA and a Manna way of looking at things—a different philosophy and perspective. We raise them up into levels of ministry, lay leadership and eventually into preparation for ministry at a professional level based on their character and faithfulness.

The "Manna DNA" is described as "the Manna way of looking at things," including philosophy and perspectives that are in line with the Manna leadership. This is an important quality in a leader for the Manna Church, and it is most easily accomplished when they raise up leaders from within the Manna Church. The members are raised up into lay leadership ministry and, as they continue in character and faithfulness, they are prepared to enter the ministry in a pastor position.

In conclusion, I bring together the factors of church growth and signs of being an apostle when I determine the gap between the ideal and real in the NARC. The factors of church growth and signs of being an apostle will sharply expose the non-biblical understanding of the NARC's ideal in the area of interpreting Ephesians 4:11–13 as well as apostolic gifts as signs of being an apostle.

Comparison of Biblical Ecclesiology and Manna's Concept of Ecclesiology

When compared to the biblical criteria of ecclesiology in Table 2, Manna Church agrees with; making disciples (2), presenting God's attributes (6), intimate community (7), and loving family without hierarchical order (12).

The Manna Church highly values "close" atmosphere as a big family, which is one of the biblical criteria for the church as an intimate community.

Because Fletcher is against hierarchical order between the leadership and the members of Manna, the environment of Manna demonstrates a loving family without hierarchical order in terms of operating cell groups and relating to one another on a daily basis. The Manna congregation often uses the expression "discipleship" such as "Sunday 6am Fletcher's discipleship group," "one of the pastors discipled me," "my discipleship leader helped me," and "Fletcher is an excellent discipler." The Manna congregation is aware that making disciples is one of the roles of the church.

As mentioned in the demographic information section, the most important concern for the Manna's leadership for Christian life is "hosting God's presence." They seek God's presence not only in the Sunday service, but also in their everyday lives. To Fletcher, without God's presence, he would not make any single move.

Although the Manna Church has strong aspects of being a biblical church, they fail to portray two aspects of being a church; in the area of being mission-minded and exercising spiritual gifts. First from Table 2, in regard to being mission-minded, the biblical ecclesiology strongly advocates missionary work (1), preaching and healing (4), participating in God's mission (5), doing mission led by Holy Spirit (9), inviting extended family (10), sending out as a pioneer (16), and breaking ground (17). Secondly, biblical ecclesiology also points to exercising gifts to overcome the hierarchical concept of understanding and relating to each other (14), and equipping saints by using spiritual gifts (15). Although Manna emphasizes releasing leaders and empowering people to be cell leaders, Manna fails to stir up spiritual gifts among them. They train people to be a leader, and equip saints, not by using spiritual gifts, but using their natural talents, hobbies, and special areas of interest in their lives.

New Characteristics of Apostolic Ministry at Manna Church

In comparison to Wagner's ideal understanding of the nine characteristics of the NARC, I identify new characteristics of apostolic ministry reflected through the Manna Church. This will help to determine the gap between the ideal and the real as it pertains to the Manna Church in the context of the broader NARC movement.

Apostolic Ministry is Relationally Driven

Fletcher believes that it is wrong to treat people with control, legalism, or domination in terms of exercising apostolic leadership. The emphasis is on relationships as he describes in the following:

> [Apostolic ministry] is not positional, it's relational. By relational I mean that I'm connected to you—not that I pastor you, but that we're connected. I know you, and you know me. You say, 'I need help,' and I come to help you—to the degree that you open the door and ask for my help, you have given me the authority to help you in that space. My team says it is relational because I know that to build a godly step, we have to choose to be relational.

Relational means that the leader knows his or her people at a personal level. There is reciprocity in this sense of "I know you, and you know me." As they know each other, one is free to open his or her heart and seek help, thus giving the authority to the leader to step into that place. Fletcher firmly believes that this is the way to build the ministry.

Apostolic Ministry Helps People Exercise God's Grace

The concept of "exercising God's grace" is the most foundational characteristic of Fletcher's ministry. He explains how most people don't know how to remove themselves from the law. He said, "They, apostolic leaders, have a vision . . . that is how they are controlling. Numbers don't really matter, but they are stuck in a place where they do not know how to cast the vision."

Church as God's Dwelling Place

Fletcher points to the lack of biblical understanding of the church as God's dwelling place: He asserts that we need to go back to the Bible in terms of structuring the church. He has heard people talk about "visitation from God" but he discusses the need for us to become the "perpetual dwelling places for God" where God "lives, not just visits." He clarifies that he is not against laying on of hands and people falling down and receiving the impartation, but he is concerned about leaving that place and returning to a "dry and parched state of spiritual death" during which one waits for the next visitation. He elaborates:

> If we build this thing biblically, with a passion for God, a passion for souls, and a passion for His work, He will come and it won't be as high as a mountain top experience. I'm preaching to the choir, I know. You know in a movie when there is real high intensity, they have to put in some humorous moments because no one can sustain that level of pressure throughout the whole movie. We had a renewal but it was eventually becoming inward, so I eventually had to end it. Not take away the Holy Spirit but I told the folks, "Look if this is of the Holy Spirit it will always end up in winning the lost, and if it doesn't, we missed it." We shifted it from "we are going to come here and pray for you" to "be filled till you have been filled here, and now we are going to shift our efforts to sending you out and going into the community." It worked.

In order for the church to become a dwelling place for God, the church needs to be built according to how God wants it. The ingredients for the continual presence of God are "passion for God, a passion for souls, and a passion for his work." This means the church should not concentrate on inward growth but focus on outreach to the community. When he felt that the church was turning more inward, he shifted the focus from praying for one another to "sending out and going into the community." Unless there is the salvation for the lost, the church would miss the criteria for his dwelling presence. Once the shift occurred, he felt that his church was able to carry on the dwelling presence of God.

Planting Churches as Multi-Site Campuses

One of the new characteristics of the NARC is the way to plant churches in an urban setting. Fletcher differentiates between two generations: baby boomers and generation X, in their preference on how the church is built. Baby boomers are into "sleek, exciting experiences." They are more into a "new way of packaging the truth to please themselves." Generation X, is "into experience because they don't trust sleek and smooth." They are interested in what Fletcher calls "vintage Christianity" where they create the experience by lighting candles with some stained glass. With these differences in preferences, the older generation church is unable to reach the younger generation. The largest growing population in his church is age group eighteen to thirty-year old. The danger with this age group is that they believe they can construct a church whatever way they want. However, these different styles of worship are not important to Fletcher. He emphasizes the importance of the Holy Spirit in these worship services:

> Churches that do not embrace the power of the Holy Spirit have to create some type of mechanism to mimic his presence. . . . It's the version of Christianity that says, "I can construct a church however I want to." No, you need to build it the way God said to build it. If you build on his presence, when people walk through the door they will say "I'm not sure what this is." My passion is that if you make God happy, he will take care of the rest—no weirdness but let's focus on the presence.

Fletcher explains the reason for having a multi-site service; that is, one church, but many different locations in the city. "It's a different way of going to church. Who says that they all have to meet in one spot? We have planted churches in this region but once we have planted, we give them the freedom to do whatever they need to do."

He continues to explain the practical way of doing a multi-site community of believers. Currently, his church is in the process of acquiring another building. Once established, Fletcher plans to drive to the new building from the current building, "like Jack Hayford did." Through this, he plans to have everything "live." It will be a satellite service with live worship, live announcements, and live altar call. He dispels the notion that everyone needs to meet in the same place for church worship. Cell groups will be based on what the church is already doing. He projects the church to grow to 6,000–7,000 people.

Growth Factors for an Apostolic Church

Fletcher sums up the growth factors for church with four points: The Kingdom of God, an understanding of destiny, an environment of grace, and an outreach culture.

> Understanding that we are not here for ourselves but we are here to do something on the planet that was God's planet from the beginning, we are here to do things for the Kingdom of God. . . . As an individual church member, I have a calling on my life. I am responsible to work that out through giftedness, abilities, and talents. Secondly, I have a corporate calling. Since I cannot get there by myself, my destiny is connected to the person beside me and on the other side; and together we have a corporate destiny. . . .

Legalism kills. I think that an environment of grace is the breath, the wind, and the life of a believer . . . creating a congregational lifestyle as an outreach culture through forming cells based on their own hobby and their own talent.

Fletcher, believes that the most important job for him is to set a strategy and help others discover their calling by motivating, inspiring, and depositing faith in them. His main focus for leadership training is to cast vision, raise faith, discover destiny, and help others to understand the meaning of grace. For Fletcher, the growth factor for the Apostolic Church is to understand the Kingdom of God, understand destiny, create grace, and be an outreach to the community. Thus, his ministry focus is, through his teaching and training, to impart understanding, inspiration, and faith to the leaders to attain these growth factors.

Determining the Gap between the Ideal and Reality

In this section I analyze the data I just presented in order to identify the gap between the ideal and the reality in Manna Church. In Table 7, I show a comparison between the Manna Church's reality with that of Wagner's ideal of the NARC. I drew data from interviewing Fletcher's congregation members and his apostolic team members. Manna's understanding of ministry exemplifies certain areas of Wagner's theory to be practiced more strongly than others.

Out of the nine characteristics of NARC from Wagner's criteria, Manna Church shows three agreed, four disagreed, and two none of the above. In addition to the nine characteristics of the NARC, Manna demonstrates four new characteristics of NARC which is related to the areas of releasing cell leaders based on grace, planting multi-site campuses in the same city as the mother church, relationally driven leadership, and the church as God's dwelling place. These four new characteristics went beyond Wagner's nine characteristics.

Table 7

The Gap between Ideal and Reality in Case One

Wagner's Ideal Characteristics for a New Apostolic Ministry	Manna's Reality Compared with Wagner's	
	Agreed or Disagreed with Wagner Characteristics	*New*
Having a "new" name to distinguish themselves from others	N/A	N/A
New authority structure led by "charismatic" pastor-leaders who have a vision for what people can become	Disagreed: An apostle called as a senior pastor. The pastoral team structured like any other denomination church.	An apostle as a nurturing mother
Strong leadership training and lay ministries	Disagreed: The discipleship training and cell leaders training like similar as a traditional church.	Exercise grace to empower the saints
New ministry focus	Agreed: Strong sense of vision and future	Impartation of gifts
New worship style.	Agreed: Focus on God's presence	N/A
New prayer forms; earnest in prayer	Disagreed: No specific indication.	N/A
New financing	N/A	N/A
New outreach; compassion for the lost; many ministries to the unchurched	Disagreed: Evangelism occurs as one of church activities.	Planting multi-site church in the local.
New power priorities; passion for the outpouring of God's Spirit.	Agreed: Focusing on hosting God's presence in the church.	Church as a God's dwelling place

Case Study One: Manna Church

Based on the review of Wagner's nine indicators of NARC, the strengths that partially fulfill the indicators for the Manna Church, Fayetteville, North Carolina, are: first, in its new ministry focus; second, in new worship style; and third, in new power priorities. Regarding the new ministry focus, Manna Church values vision as one of the crucial elements of the Christian life. As Wagner states, "NARC starts with the present situation and focuses on the future."[12] Manna seeks a vision from their leadership, and the most important job for the leadership is to cast the vision into members' lives.

As far as new worship style is concerned, Manna Church seeks God's presence during praise worship by pouring out their heart with enthusiasm. They invite the Holy Spirit while they worship and praise God and express their emotion freely. This also relates directly to the area of new power priorities. Manna believes that the church needs to be God's dwelling place. They focus on hosting God's presence during the Sunday service. These are the three new indicators that can be seen as indicators of a healthy church within NARC.

The gap between Wagner's ideal and the Manna reality lies in four different areas: (1) New authority structure led by "charismatic" pastor-leader who has a vision for what people can become; (2) Strong leadership training and lay ministries; (3) New prayer forms; and (4) New outreach.

First Gap: New Authority Structure

Wagner's understanding of NARC's new authority structure emphasizes charismatic leadership meaning that an apostolic leader will be recognized by the spiritual anointing.[13] However, the first gap is that Manna's authority structure stresses "grace" rather than "charismatic." Fletcher believes that an apostle of biblical authority is to be a nurturing mother who releases the children by exercising grace.

Second Gap: Leadership Training

The second gap between Wagner's ideal and Manna's reality is in the area of training strong lay leadership. According to Wagner, NARC pastoral

---

12. Wagner, *New Apostolic Reformation Church*, 21.
13. Wagner, *New Apostolic Reformation Church*, 20.

leadership is home grown without traditional seminary training.[14] In reality, the majority of Manna's hired pastoral staff have degrees from a traditional seminary. Fletcher also works very well with elders which are in contrast with Wagner's ideal of the absence of nominating committees.[15]

Third Gap: New Prayer Forms

The third gap shows in the area of new prayer forms. Compared to the traditional church, Wagner believes the worship service of the NARC exceeds the amount of time spent on prayer.[16] Although Manna seeks God's presence during worship, there are no indications of distinctive prayer time during the worship service.

Fourth Gap: New Outreach

The fourth gap between Wagner's ideal and reality is identified in the area of new outreach. Wagner insists that a strong characteristic of the NARC is in helping the unfortunate people, the disadvantaged, and the handicapped as a new form of outreach.[17] He believes that this can be applied as both evangelism and mission. However, Manna's evangelism is limited to the department of "prayer and evangelism" rather than demonstrating a strong sense of compassion for the poor.

Chapter 6 presents the data from the second case study, the Word of Life Church in Red Deer, Alberta, Canada and Apostle Mel Mullen.

---

14. Wagner, *New Apostolic Reformation Church*, 21.
15. Wagner, *New Apostolic Reformation Church*, 21.
16. Wagner, *New Apostolic Reformation Church*, 23.
17. Wagner, *New Apostolic Reformation Church*, 24.

Chapter 6

Case Study Two: Word of Life Church

THE WORD OF LIFE Church (WOLC) is located in Red Deer, Alberta, Canada. The church was founded by Apostle Mel Mullen in 1972. Mullen is an overseer of "Business Leader's Network" and the "Canadian Prayer Network." The interview data was taken from twelve pastoral team members out of fifteen. The duration of gathering data was from May 26, 2007 to May 31, 2007.

Demographic Information

The city of Red Deer is centrally located between the two major cities of Calgary and Edmonton. The city economy consists of a growing manufacturing industry, alongside the retail and wholesale service industry. Most residents were born in the province or within Canada. Most of the immigrants residing in Red Deer are from Asia, the Middle East, and South and Central America. The Philippines is first among the top ten countries in terms of immigrants.

The WOLC consists of six extension churches, one Christian school, one Bible college, and Wagner Leadership Institute. WOLC fifteen pastoral team members include the senior pastor, executive pastor, assistant pastor, family pastor, worship pastor, children's pastor, and accountant administrator. Each pastor has a mentor group that consists of eighteen people and meets once a month. These are people selected based on their leadership potential and cohesive groupings.

Definition of Apostleship from Mullen and WOLC Congregation

According to Mullen,[1] the definition of apostle is one who provides an "apostolic covering" as described in Acts 13. He described how Paul and Barnabas were sent out by the Holy Spirit with a laying on of hands to plant churches. They went all over, and basically, they planted local indigenous churches. They had an apostolic covering, but most of the time they could not reach their apostle because they were a long distance away and couldn't communicate. As reported by a pastoral team member, the WOLC recognizes Mullen as an apostle for his leadership over the apostle's coalition and as a spiritual covering. He is also recognized for his prophetic gift, accompanied by signs, wonders, and miracles. Following is one testimony: "Pastor Mel is apostolic for sure, in the sense that he oversees leadership and gives direction, not just in the city but also in the nation and in the world. I think that it's something that God has instilled in him."

The data from Mullen's congregation emphasize the spiritual anointing of apostleship that does not match any part of the biblical definition. The spiritual anointing is expressed as apostolic covering that is manifested in the area of planting churches as reported by one pastor of an extension church:

> I wouldn't pastor that church [extension church of WOLC] on my own. I would not feel capable, and none of it would happen. I just wouldn't do it. But I think it's from the empowering model; the one that takes people up and puts them on levels where they probably shouldn't be. But because of the support system they are able to do these things.

The data from Mullen's congregation emphasize the spiritual anointing of apostleship that does not match with any of the biblical definitions. For the WOLC, the spiritual anointing is expressed as apostolic covering that is manifested in the area of planting churches.

Similar to Cannistraci's view of apostleship, the WOLC makes the observation that formed a definition of apostle as a spiritual covering. Cannistraci defined an apostle as "one who is called and sent by Christ to have the spiritual authority, character, gifts, and abilities to successfully reach and establish people in kingdom truth and order, especially through

---

1. Mullen, personal interview with author, 2009.

founding and overseeing local churches."[2] Although the WOLC agrees with Cannistraci's definition of apostleship, the WOLC's focus lies in the spiritual anointing of the apostle rather than the apostle being an ambassador.[3] This contrast is also observed in Wagner's view of apostle as a missionary.

Definition of the Apostolic Role from Mullen and WOLC Congregation

The role of apostleship, based on the interview data from the WOLC, can be identified in four different areas: casting vision, empowering and releasing people, being a final authority, and being a father figure.

Casting Vision

The first role of apostle is about casting vision. They believe that the primary role of the apostle is to cast vision for the church, and the rest of the pastoral leadership and congregation carry out the apostle's vision. One of the pastors explained that the main reason for him to be a pastoral team member is to carry out the apostle Mullen's vision for the house. This is accomplished when one understands and grasps the leader's heart, as reported:

> Grasping the leader's heart is most important so that you can react the same way that they would react if you had to cover a situation for them. That's very critical, trying to figure out why they think the way they do and what is the passion and vision. Then they know that they can give you something and you will respond with their heart. In training other people if I can teach them how to think instead of just telling them what to do, it's when we are successful.

Because of the support that the leaders feel from Mullen, the leaders are "full onboard with him in whatever direction he takes." They see that the vision Mullen shares is not just an idea but it is "a word from God," and he will have a strategy to implement it. These are considered all part of the role of the apostle. The leaders find their job to be "keeping up" with the apostle. "Mullen empowers me and gives me leeway to do what needs to

---

2. Cannistraci, *Gift of Apostle*, 26.
3. Cannistraci, *Gift of Apostle*, 26.

be done. The things that God gives you to run with, they are really behind what you're doing; my greatest job is to keep up with Pastor Mel."

Empowering and Releasing People

The second role as an apostle is that of empowering and releasing people. This was done when Mullen released younger people to "decide what things were going to be done." As the younger generation responded, it changed the worship; a change in music, use of media, and shorter sermons. This resulted in a positive atmosphere in which people want to come to church more as a result. In line with empowering and releasing, Mullen sees his apostolic role in being a "mentor or coach." Mullen explains the reason for his releasing the younger generation:

> You have to release them. It's what we did at some point, release everybody into their call. They are so gifted. What we did differently is that we started to listen to them. We actually did what they wanted instead of doing what we wanted. We realized that we need to change instead of them changing. They can reach generation. They can reach the culture. So now we are encouraging them to get people, and they start releasing. We don't want it to die when we die, which has been a problem for years in the church. There is a great church but when the founder dies the ministry dies. We don't want that. We want to go on. We want to create more spaces for them. That's where we feel our calling is—to create places for them.

As the younger generation was released, although they did not feel experienced or mature enough to do the job well, they felt supported in all that they did. Here is one testimony:

> I think that Pastor Mel released us to do our jobs. They had an inexperienced team, but they just believed in us. They came alongside. For instance, in my job, I would have to make many decisions and they trusted me with the decisions, and if I did something that they didn't like or didn't work out, then we would just change it. It wasn't a big deal. You felt more released to do your job. Also to grow in your leadership. And I think that made a huge difference. Just the freedom that they gave us and also (they) took their hands off from a lot of things. They acknowledged and respected us as leaders and respected our choices and our opinions about things.

Case Study Two: Word of Life Church

One of the ways the younger generation was supported was by "modeling." The pastoral leaders are committed to training up the next generation as explained:

> We model everything we do. I started a men's group. I had a guy in my men's group that I wanted him to run the group. So, what I did was I trained him for two years in the mentorship group and this year I said, "Bro' are you ready to start this on your own?" And he said, "Yes, I'm ready to do it." Basically, you walk them through and show them how to do it and then you go, "Here, this is yours." Then once a week, I made a commitment to him, that we would go get some coffee. He gives me an update. Usually I let him open up his heart first then I check on him. I love empowering others. The media room is filled with young people being empowered to run those cameras. It's important because we just can't do all those areas. We have to empower people.

The empowering and releasing allows the congregation to be equipped and trained to use their gifts. For example, when someone raises a hand for healing, the congregation around the individual is asked to put their hands on the person and pray for the healing. This allows them, in turn, to go out into the community and exercise their gifts as they have done in the church.

Being a Final Authority

The third role of an apostle from WOLC is that the apostle is the one who gets the word from God. This is related to the apostle as "first in rank" in governing authority. Mullen expresses his main role as apostle is to be responsible for the final decisions. He sees that the "final authority" in the church matters, therefore the ultimate responsibility, rests in him. He helps the member churches make decisions for buying property, training leaders, etc. He repeats: "Ultimately my responsibility is that, the final authority in those churches rests in me."

Mullen insists the strong authority of apostolic ministry is necessary for an effective ministry today. He embodies a hierarchical form of leadership as an effective equipping tool for his congregation. In agreement with Mullen, one of pastoral leadership expresses the benefit of having an apostle as strong authority to "get things done." They strongly believe that the mandate comes from the apostle, as stated in Ephesians:

> The apostle isn't the only gift there. The apostle is mentioned first because it's more of a governmental thing. Most apostles that I have been around want answers quickly and they want to get things done. That doesn't mean that the other gifts are less important. It just means that their role is. I think the biggest thing for a teacher, evangelist, minister, what is important to see is that the apostolic gift isn't a greater gift, but its role is very significant—more of a significant role because it brings it all together and helps those other people.

Father Figure

Lastly, WOLC sees the apostle as a father figure. It is leadership with a "father's heart." It is a heart that cares about others in a personal way as stated:

> So it's not just a business relationship, but there is leadership with a father heart—like a heart that cares about the longevity of things and the community of things. It's not self-focused, but it's about building something for God.

The data from Mullen and the WOLC congregation strongly disagree with (26) of Table 1 in relation to the "first rank." Gordon Fee claims that in 1 Corinthians 12:28, "first of all" is interpreted not as "first rank,"[4] but as a chronological sense of "first" when an apostle accomplishes the role of "pioneering church."[5] Agreeing with Fee, Raymond F. Collins explains that the connotation of "first of all" has no relation to the first rank.[6] Vander Broek has a final word for "first of all" in 1 Corinthians 12:28 as "simply corresponding to the chronological appearance in the context."[7]

The understanding of the role of apostle from Mullen and the WOLC congregation agrees with Wagner and John Kelly. Wagner defines the main role of apostle as "to cast vision for the church."[8] John Kelly describes an apostle as a spiritual father figure saying, "our success should be measured by the quality of the sons and daughters whom we are preparing for."[9]

---

4. Fee, *First Epistle to the Corinthians*, 619.
5. Fee, *First Epistle to the Corinthians*, 620.
6. Collins, *First Corinthians*, 468.
7. Vander Broek, *Breaking Barriers*, 133.
8. Wagner, *Apostles and Prophets*, 33.
9. Kelly, *End Time Warriors*, 13.

Case Study Two: Word of Life Church

Understanding of Apostolic-Concept from Mullen and WOLC Congregation

The WOLC congregation understands that the strength of having apostolic leadership is being able to sustain a long-term relationship in a local church setting. They believe that the apostolic leaders stay in the local church much longer than other denominational leaders. One of the pastoral leaders expressed his understanding:

> Structure is good. Because, as you look at the statistics of pastors in Canada, eighteen months is the average one pastor stays in one location. One of five main things that were important for transformation was the leadership. The structure of the church at large, in most cases, is really not allowing leadership to last. One person who I look up to is Bill who has been at one location for a long period of time and looks at what he could do. We look at whose ministry is growing. You see who has made a difference in their community. You look at long-lasting leadership. Some of these churches you see the youth group rising up from nothing to 75 and when they (the youth leader) leave, then there is nothing and you have to start all over again. All of a sudden you see that the people have a hard time attaching themselves to the man of God because why would you attach yourself when you know he is going to be gone. People are leaving because of leadership leaving.

The WOLC's perspective on how an apostle works within a local church is to equip people as a team. The apostolic team consists of a prophet, teacher, evangelist, and pastor. One leader explains:

> I think that pastors need to recognize their gift as well. Teachers need to do that as well. I'm a teacher, and I don't have the gift of evangelist—well, I do, but it's not my strongest gift. But I value the person that is an evangelist. And if I'm not a pastor, then, I value that person who is a pastor. I have more of an apostle mindset but I am not an apostle but I have that mindset more than a pastor mindset. But I need pastors because if I don't have pastors the apostle mindset will just knock people over. The gifting of the church is there to equip the saints for ministry.... The best thing a leader can do is to create jobs for other people.

In terms of apostolic authority, they strongly believe that the apostolic anointing is transferable. When one receives impartation from someone else with apostolic gifting, one can walk into that gifting. The following is how they believe Mullen received his apostolic anointing:

> He [Mullen] put himself in a place where (there were) people with apostolic gifting, like I think at one time he [Mullen] was just a pastor. I think he received gifting through impartation from people like Peter Wagner. I don't think Mullen was born as an apostle. You recognize the gift that is in you, but there is a prophet and that gift is worked on for a long season of time, often time, it is in private. All of a sudden it's through impartation. Through that whole time, God keeps growing it.

Lastly, one way that the WOLC understands the apostolic concept is how apostolic leadership focuses on the transformation of society. Mullen reports that the WOLC has been running conferences all across Canada. They carried the theme of the "apostle movement." They have taken a leadership role for the Apostolic Movement and built a network in Canada. Now there is a group of apostles that meet regularly. Some of these conferences were called Impact Cities with "reformation" as a theme. The mission was to build local churches to "transform cities and nations." One leader put it this way:

> One of our goals right now is to talk to people that might be Catholic, etc. That's one of our main goals. We want righteousness in the land. To me, that's very apostolic. If I could describe it, I would say, that's very apostolic. That [is a] passion of not just trying to make his church a better place but to make the nation a better place. It's a generational church but very much apostolic.

The concept of apostle from Mullen and the WOLC agrees with (33) of Table 1, a tool to equip the church. Among the four main concepts from Mullen and the WOLC congregation, three concepts of apostleship are new compared to the biblical criteria.

Although three concepts cannot be identified from the biblical understanding of apostleship, the "transformation of society" aspect can be found in Wagner's criteria. Wagner states: "Those participating in the new wineskin of the Second Apostolic Age continue aggressive evangelism and church planting, but they also pray for and work toward the transformation of society."[10] What he emphasizes here is that the transformation of society is an important characteristic of NARC as much as evangelism and

---

10. Wagner, *Changing Church*, 93.

church planting. In a similar line of thinking, Wagner believes that when we acknowledge "marketplace apostles" just like the church apostles, an explosive transformation will occur in all levels of society.[11] He strongly believes in the relation between the apostle and social transformation.

Ecclesiology in the WOLC

In this section, I describe six characteristics of the WOLC as ecclesiology. These six characteristics are compared with the nine characteristics of Wagner's criteria for NARC in order to identify a gap between the ideal and reality.

Ephesus Model

According to the WOLC leadership, in the past, they built churches following a model of indigenous local churches, also called "satellite" churches. However, as the churches met on different campuses, the DNA of the WOLC was lost. Then, they decided to try a different approach using the Ephesus model, where it is one church in many locations. They found that this model keeps the DNA of the WOLC and called the model an "extension church." The advantage of this type of church was explained:

> When you walk into the church of Act Ville, it should feel like home. It should feel very similar because it's the same spirit, music; we believe the same things, and we have the same programs. It's very good because you have a group of about thirty to fifty people and its good, but we can do so much more with more resources and more people. Isn't it great when a pastor isn't on his own, and he is not alone; where he has a full team of people, and he has someone he is being covered by—someone in authority over him? So it's very empowering because instead of being isolated, alone in this place, where you know they need God pretty badly—you know it's quite a battle—you fight it with the help of your friends.

There are various ways to form the extension church. One way is through Emerging Church. Below is one testimony:

> Our congregation actually began in the community, and through some problems that happened in the church, they turned to Mel

---

11. Wagner, *Apostles and Prophets*, 55.

for some guidance. Since that time that church has always been an extension of this church. Because since that time when the church went through some trouble—in the mid 1980s—the pastor has always been part of this church.

Relational Based Church

Mullen explains that there was a time, in the earlier days, when WOLC was "program based." Then, as WOLC moved to a "relational-based" church, they intentionally changed everything including the music and the length of the service. As the church emphasized reaching out to the lost souls, they began to see many first-generation Christians (new converts, who are in need of relationships). Thus, the ministry became "relational." The staff worked as a group with the common goal of building relationships with one another as well as building relationships with these new converts. They emphasized that there are no "stars" but they all do "great things."

> If anything is built on structure with no relationship, it's not going to work. Everything is built on relationship. With my team, I'm not just building structure—even though I do build structure—I'm building people and relationships. Structure should always come afterwards. . . . If you try to structure things before you relate to them, it won't work. When you are building a person you think about what does a person need? They need support, they need to learn, need worship, and need prayer. You need to provide that atmosphere and then watch that person grow. You can grow things fast. But I see that in some churches like I see it, they try to grow a turkey with steroids—it grows fast but when you take a bite it's not healthy.

Even though some people drop out, there are still a good number of people who remain that have a one-on-one relationship. Without relationships, they would not have remained.

Building Church for the Next Generation as Evangelistic Strategy

According to Mullen, in 2004, the church began a transition from a "renewal-model church" to a "city-reaching church." The church "turned the arrows from inside to out." He continued to bring a focus that the church called itself, "charismatic, faith, restoration, prayer, apostolic, prophetic, marketplace, city reaching" and was also for the next generation. He believes that it has gone beyond all of its history for the next generation, and it is now a "tri-generational" church.

The WOLC pastoral leaders recognized that there has been a problem in many churches in that when the founder of a great church died, the ministry also died. They did not want that to happen to the WOLC. They wanted to create more space for the next generation. They felt that it was their calling to create places for them. In the process, they recognized that they needed to change themselves instead of changing the younger generation. They recognized that the younger generation can reach the present generation and present culture. Therefore, they started to listen to the younger generation and did what they wanted instead of having them change. As they found the younger generation to be "so gifted," they were released into their calling. This process was "very intense" and took six to nine months. Now, the older generation is excited to see the next generation, even to the fourth generation in the church, being released as leaders.

As the church made changes for the younger generation, this was communicated to the entire congregation by Mullen for many months. He spoke to the general congregation that things would be different; that there were going to be "lights and smoke," which are the kinds of things that the older generations "do not know what to do with." The need for the change was clearly communicated. The result is that the older generation became just as happy and excited about the changes. Their attendance increased as well.

The main goal of the generation church is seeing people get saved. They want the church to be "genuine and functional" and reach the culture. They feel that this is God's heart as well. The disconnection with the next generation in Canadian churches occurred when the older pastors turned over the churches to younger pastors. Since the latter did not have "the same thoughts" as the former, the church would lose its focus. Even when the apostles in Canada gathered and made some declarations for the church, they realized that it was not for the next generation. They realized that most churches have created cultures of their own that will no longer reach the culture of mainstream society. Thus, the culture of the church became no longer relevant. Therefore, the importance of releasing the next generation to "run the show" became evident. This releasing and emphasizing the next generation also became their evangelistic strategy to reach out to peoples in the community.

Decision Made Through Fasting, Praying, and Hearing

For the WOLC, at the beginning of each year, there is a time of corporate prayer in which they seek to hear from God and share with the apostle what they believe they are hearing from God. Once there is an agreement, the apostle shares the vision with all the other churches. These are usually confirmed by the other church leaders as well.

One of the results of making decisions through fasting, praying, and hearing is that the leadership team pursues the direction of the next emphasis of ministry. Mullen described, "Recently, there was a time of fasting and praying and listening to God. He felt the Lord telling him that the era of transformation conferences is complete." He felt the Lord telling him, "You have done the job." Based on him hearing from God, WOLC shifted their ministry focus.

Focus on Holy Spirit

According to Mullen, the main force of apostolic ministry is the Holy Spirit. There is an emphasis on the "passion for outpouring of the Holy Spirit" often in terms of praying, worshipping, and doing missions. Mullen states that whenever he needs a new direction for his ministry, he seeks guidance from the Holy Spirit. His team also strongly believes that the mark of apostolic ministry is to recognize the Holy Spirit's presence and an outpouring of the Holy Spirit in people's hearts.

New Leadership Training

The process of being a pastoral leader can be described as "grassroots growing." The grassroots growing method is to select pastoral leaders of the Apostolic Church within the church setting rather than selecting from outside resources such as seminary educated pastor. Here are two pastoral leadership cases that show "grassroots growing:"

> I was a church member who went to Bible College and then came to a Bible school as an administrator, which is one of my strengths. I worked at the Bible school for three-to-four years and had demonstrated the ability to run the program. So when the opportunity came, I was considered because of the track record of what I had been [doing] at the Bible school. That's how

Case Study Two: Word of Life Church

> I transitioned from a member of a congregation to becoming a pastor.[12]

> I'm an executive pastor and I have been on staff since 1996. For eleven years. I went to Bible school here and then Pastor Mel took me on six years ago to train me for the executive job.[13]

WOLC has a strong sense of the church as a loving family. They relate with each other like a father relates with his son in order to develop a relationship in depth. The family analogy is described by one leader:

> Sometimes we also recognize that there is a strong link, and one of the pictures that I use to describe the link of our churches is families. Naturally, in any family, there is the mother, father, sons, daughters—and our church is like a son or daughter church. And even in a natural family, no matter how old I get, I still have my parents. Because you're older or mature, it doesn't mean that you don't need your parents or you throw them away. As our church grows and matures it's the same as in a family. We have a father and a mother. . . . It's organic like a family. As a son grows, he will have his own house.

Compare Biblical Ecclesiology and WOLC's Ecclesiology

In comparison with Table 2, WOLC agrees with the numbers (7) intimate community; (9) doing mission led by the Holy Spirit; (11) operate under the direct influence of the Holy Spirit; (14) exercising gifts to hurdle the hierarchical concept of understanding and relating to each other; and (15) equipping the saints by using spiritual gifts.

The most remarkable thing that the WOLC demonstrates is that they have an intimate community in the area of relating and working together as a pastoral team. The intimate pastoral leadership community demonstrates the fruit of empowering and releasing leaders. The demographics of 90 percent of the pastor leaders being under thirty years of age is significant. The young pastoral leaders are a demonstration of Mullen's belief that can be summed up as creating a church for the next generation. All the three areas are tied together to create the unique characteristics of the WOLC: (1) intimate pastoral community; (2) exercising gifts to hurdle the hierarchical

---

12. See page 211 for case study 13.
13. See page 211 for case study 15.

concept of understanding and relating to each other; and (3) building a church for the next generation by releasing and empowering young pastoral leadership.

However, there is an important factor that cannot be overlooked in the pastoral team. Most of the young pastoral leaders are either direct family members of Mullen or relatives of Mullen. The assistant pastor, family pastor, and worship pastor are Mullen's family, as are the children's pastor, and the WLI leadership, all relatives of Mullen. This data behind-the-scene clearly speaks of the limitation of the three characteristics of the WOLC. Moreover, these three characteristics are manifested in pastoral leadership rather than in the WOLC congregation.

In terms of the emphasis on the Holy Spirit, the WOLC leadership highly values hearing from the Holy Spirit whenever they make ministry decisions such as direction, doing mission, and selecting leaders. In the biblical ecclesiology, the Holy Spirit's guidance is directly related to God's mission. However, the WOLC's emphasis on the Holy Spirit is for the purpose of maintaining strong leadership rather than participating in God's mission. The WOLC seeks evangelism through their extension churches. However, they fail to demonstrate the biblical ecclesiology in terms of being missional in the community and proclaiming the Kingdom of God in everyday congregational lives. The weakest point of the WOLC lies in their indifference to taking their ministry beliefs to the next level. It means that the pastoral team is equipped by Mullen alone as the apostle. However, the WOLC congregation is not equipped as much as the pastoral leadership. The WOLC congregation is not aware of apostolic gifts and has a general lack of knowledge in the area of equipping the saints.

New Characteristics of Apostolic Ministry in the WOLC

The WOLC demonstrates characteristics that are not included in the Wagner's criteria of apostolic churches. I discuss here six distinctive characteristics of apostolic ministry in the WOLC.

Not Openly Using Apostolic Terminology

Mullen tries to use vocabulary and terminology that "the world understands" such as "mentor" or "coaching," instead of "apostolic" or "prophetic." He tries to use language that people will understand and can relate with.

Case Study Two: Word of Life Church

However, in conferences, terms like apostolic or prophetic are freely used since everyone there is considered a Christian. He expressed his opinion about the terminology: "The only thing I have to say is that I don't think the terms are important. The funny thing is that there has been so much talk about the word apostle. I have been to the ICA (International Council of Apostles), and it doesn't matter."

Model of the Book of Acts

Mullen discussed the Jerusalem church as described in Acts 2. The Jerusalem Church is for the city. He also calls it "city vision" and states that this is "the least vision" any person should have. Then, he discussed the Ephesian Church as described in Acts 19. This church was "unique because it was a church for the province of Asia in many locations." This gave Mullen a model to work from. He is now working on planting a church in India where the members are not a local indigenous congregation, but "an extension" of his church.[14]

As he plants churches in India, Turkey, or 100 other different locations, they can be one church in multiple locations. He hopes that, eventually, these churches will connect to the WOLC on the internet and join the staff meetings on the Internet. They have already done that with some churches, talking over the telephone, and then on the Internet. He calls this "Acts 19, one church in many locations." At the time of our conversation, they were planting churches in Rwanda, Istanbul, and India. There are about twenty churches on the Acts 19 principle.

Individual Destiny as Related to Local Church Destiny

The WOLC takes the destiny of their lives seriously. They value a corporate sense of destiny as a whole, as well as that of an individual. They believe that the relationship between the corporate destiny of a local church and the individual's destiny are closely connected with one another. The leadership of WOLC insists:

---

14. Although Mullen indicates that his way of planting churches is based on Acts 19, NT model of apostolic church does not consider the church member as the members of his own church.

Your purpose and destiny are wrapped up in the vision of that church. So whether you are called to be a dentist, pastor, or work for McDonald's, you have your part to play in building the local church. When you have more people fulfilling their purpose, feeling released and functioning in what they were called to do, then you just get a lot of happy people who are excited about life and excited about partnering with a vision that is bigger than them.

Global Perspective

Mullen makes a conscious effort to present to the church a "bigger perspective beyond just the local church, but for the city and the nation." The attempt to take the church outside of its walls is done consciously every Sunday. This is also accomplished by Mullen visiting other nations—several different nations a year. He has been to Germany, India, Istanbul, Africa, Jamaica, and "all over the place" together with his team.

Determining the Gap between the Ideal and the Reality

In this section, I will analyze the data I presented in this chapter in order to identify the gap between the ideal and the reality in the WOLC. In Table 8, I present a comparison of WOLC's reality as a NARC, with that of Wagner's ideal. I drew data from interviewing Mullen's congregational members and his apostolic team members. The WOLC's understanding of ministry exemplifies certain areas of Wagner's theory to be practiced more strongly than others.

The WOLC agrees on five (two mutual) characteristics with Wagner's criteria: (1) new authority structure; (2) new ministry focus; (3) new worship style and prayer forms; (4) new outreach; and (5) new power priorities. In addition to the nine characteristics from Wagner, the WOLC shows three new characteristics in the areas of empowering and releasing as strong leadership training. They focus on the corporate sense of destiny as well as individual destiny, and planting extension churches as Ephesus models.

Case Study Two: Word of Life Church

Table 8

Between Ideal and Reality in Case Two

Wagner's Ideal Characteristics for a New Apostolic Ministry	WOLC's reality Compared with Wagner	
	Agreed or Disagreed with Wagner	**New Characteristics**
Having a "new" name to distinguish themselves from others	Disagreed: Word of Life Church is not significant in relation to Wagner's criteria.	N/A
New authority structure led by "charismatic" pastor-leaders who have a vision for what people can become	Disagreed and Agreed: Mullen was identified as charismatic prophetic-apostle who has a vision for WOLC.	N/A
Strong leadership training and lay ministries	Disagreed and Agreed: By empowering and releasing the next generation leaders, Mullen brought strong leadership.	Empowering and releasing the next generational pastoral leadership (limited in terms of targeting Mullen's kinship)
New ministry focus	Agreed: They focus on the future of the church.	Focus on the corporate sense of destiny.
New worship style.	Agreed: Focus on the Holy Spirit while they worship.	N/A
New prayer forms; earnest in prayer	Agreed: They value fasting and praying when they make decisions.	N/A
New financing	N/A	N/A
New outreach; compassion for the lost; many ministries to the unchurched.	Agreed: Focus on the next generation as an evangelistic tool.	Doing evangelism as they plant the extension churches called Ephesus model based on global perspective.
New power priorities; passion for outpouring of God's Spirit.	Agreed: They eagerly wait on the Holy Spirit.	

The interview data from the WOLC suggest that the strength it depends on is the Holy Spirit. They stress the "passion for outpouring of the Holy Spirit" often in terms of praying, worshipping, and doing missions. Mullen insists that he seeks the Holy Spirit's counsel whenever he needs a new direction for his ministry. His team also strongly believes that the mark of apostolic ministry is to recognize the Holy Spirit's presence and outpouring of the Holy Spirit in people's hearts. His church recognizes Mullen as an apostle for his leadership over the apostle's coalition and for his prophetic gift, accompanied by signs, wonders, and miracles.

The gap between Wagner's ideal and the WOLC's reality is manifested in the areas of strong leadership training, new authority structure, and new outreach.

First Gap: Limited New Authority Structure

Apostle Mullen insists that the strong authority of apostolic ministry is necessary for an effective ministry today. He embodies a hierarchical form of leadership as an effective equipping tool for his congregation. According to Mullen, an apostle in his NARC functions as the highest office, position, or title. He believes that an apostle has absolute authority in the local church and over the network of churches. While an apostle is understood as a title and functions as one of the offices of the five-fold ministries of Ephesians 4:11, there are no other functioning offices of Ephesians 4:11 in the WOLC. That is, there is the recognition of the five-fold ministries; but in practice, only apostleship is adopted and exists to support a hierarchical, top-down structure which makes a distinction from Wagner's description. Wagner mentioned new authority structure as "a transition from bureaucratic authority to personal authority, from legal structure to relational structure, from control to coordination, and from rational leadership to charismatic leadership."[15] Although Wagner's ideal understanding of new authority structure functions in personal, relational, and coordination style, Mullen's leadership strongly demonstrates bureaucratic and controlling leadership.

For example, one of the pastoral leadership confirms Mullen's leadership saying, "The apostolic mandate comes from the apostle. The mandate does not come from the board." While structurally, the board is above an apostle in this NARC, this is seen as a structural flaw that hinders the effectiveness of the ministry. Thus, the pastoral leadership adds,

---

15. Wagner, *New Apostolic Reformation Church*, 20.

"The board is up here, and the apostle or pastor is below the board. The effectiveness is not as good because he's always under this pressure of trying to please people." In such a way, the apostle Mullen has appropriated the authority of the office of an apostle without establishing the whole of the five-fold ministry.

Second Gap: Limited Strong Leadership Training

One of the strong manifestations of Mel Mullen's ministry is the fact that he has implemented the "empowering" aspect of Wagner's earlier gift-oriented definition of "apostle."[16] However, the gap in training strong leadership is observed in terms of the majority (80 percent) of those who are empowered by Mullen, the apostle. Mullen's next generation leaders are his male, extended family members. Empowerment, thus, happens in a safe environment, rather than in an open environment. In an open environment, any gifted person is identified and trained and released to be leaders according to God-given gifts. Thus, Mullen's practice of empowering would represent a departure from Wagner's 2002 description of "apostle" as one to "establish the foundational government of the church within an assigned sphere of ministry,"[17] since those that are established are largely his family members and the establishment does not reflect the five-fold ministry.

Third Gap: Limited New Outreach

In relation to planting churches, Mullen states that he exercises boldness and apostolic faith in "coordinating and breaking boundary" which agrees with Wagner's perspective in church planting.[18] However, as shown in the interview data from one of extension church pastors, one extension church emerged from an existing church rather than breaking the boundary. This goes with Gibbs's warning about the way we bring unchurched people to the Kingdom of God.[19] He claims that the biblical way of bringing people to the Kingdom of God is not through the reconfiguration of existing

---

16. Wagner, *Apostles and Prophets*, 73.
17. Wagner, *Spheres of Authority*, 27.
18. Wagner, *Apostles and Prophets*, 73.
19. Gibbs, *Church NEXT*, 18.

churchgoers, but through effective evangelistic outreach.[20] The ideal of Wagner's perspective agrees with Gibbs. However, the reality of WOLC did not reflect the practice of the NARC's ideal.

Now, I move to the third case study, of Bethel World Outreach Center in Nashville, TN. Following this final presentation, I will compare and contrast the interrelation of my three case studies in a findings chapter.

---

20. Gibbs, *Church NEXT*, 18.

Chapter 7

Case Study Three: Bethel World Outreach Center

Bethel World Outreach Center (BWOC) is located in Brentwood, Tennessee, a suburb of Nashville. The city of Brentwood has about 35,000 population. It is 95 percent White with 1.9 percent African-American and 2.5 percent Asian. This church was founded in 1984 by Ray McCollum. Then, Rice Broocks became senior pastor of BWOC in 1993. In addition to the main congregation, the BWOC has five satellite congregations in the greater Nashville area. They raised up pastoral leadership teams and planted the five satellite services and congregations to fulfill their goal of "reaching a city to touch the world." I was able to interview seventeen of the twenty pastor leaders of this church. The duration of gathering data was first from April 30, 2007 to May 5, 2007, and then later from October 15, 2007 to October 31, 2007.

BWOC Structure

The BWOC has ten pastors and two ministers that include senior minister, executive pastor, life groups' pastor, youth pastor, children's pastors, campus pastor, associate pastors, international pastor, and music minister. The ministries include life groups and campus ministry. The BWOC is also affiliated with Every Nation Ministry. The ethnicities of the congregation members comprise Caucasian, African-American, Spanish, and Asian. One of the outstanding atmospheres about the BWOC is harmony in ethnic diversity. Compassion for the lost and ministries to the unchurched are demonstrated in their adaptation of cultural relevance to the target population.

Life Groups

The BWOC has about ninety-six small groups called life groups that meet mostly once a week across the Nashville area. The goal for the life group is spiritual growth and fellowship. The life groups can be divided into nine different categories including marriage and family groups, men's groups, women's groups, singles, youth, college, Hispanic, international, and specialty groups.

Satellite Churches

The BWOC has six different locations beginning with Bethel World Outreach Center in Brentwood, Bethel@Globe in Nashville, Bethel@Murfreesboro, Bethel Community Church@Clarksville, Bethel Community Church@Spring Hill, and Bethel Community Church@Franklin. Each church is operated by a congregational pastor and has an independent structure from the mother church.

Definition of Apostleship from Broocks and BWOC Congregation

Based on interview data from Rice Broocks[1] and the BWOC congregation, the definition of apostleship can be summed up with "being sent" for planting churches and to strengthening the existing churches. Broocks recalls his experience from the very first time he was asked to lead the BWOC by the founding pastor and realizing his apostleship:

> Sunday night, I was coming home from the meeting to the airport, and he [the founding pastor] said why don't you move to Nashville and be with me. He says that I am [Broocks] one the main disciples. . . . I traveled out here in 1993, most of my time was spent on the road either starting new churches or helping to strengthen the ones that existed.

---

1. Broocks, personal interview with the author, October 5, 2007.

Case Study Three: Bethel World Outreach Center

He continues to define apostle as a church planter:

> I was evangelistic, but mostly I was being an apostle by going to churches that were already planted and saying that they wanted to be apart of Morning Star.... It was more of an adopting. I did more adopting during those first five years than I did planting.... We did some church planting—we did some, but it was mostly me going into churches that already existed and they said we want to join you now. We were planting churches—no, it wasn't church planting. I was just being an overseer to an existing church.

He focuses the definition of apostle as "being sent" in terms of bringing in a spirit of mission.

> If somebody says to me, "What is an Apostolic Church?" I say an Apostolic Church primarily has an apostle. And what that apostle does, that spirit of "going" and "being sent" is going to be—it won't just be a government of apostles [who] now are leading—but it will be a spirit of missional. I would have used the term missional in terms of a mission-oriented focus.

Although Broocks clearly states the definition, one of the pastoral leaders discussed the limitation of apostleship in the BWOC. He explained that the apostolic is merely for leadership structure and mission strategy. What he means is that an apostle is a "sent one," who has evangelistic gifts and whose job is to extend the church borders into new areas where the Gospel has not been preached. He continues to critique that as far as he can observe in his ten years at the BWOC, the apostolic has nothing to do with the life of a congregation since the apostolic ministry is limited to evangelism and satellite church planting.

Even though the data from the BWOC agrees with the biblical definition of apostle as being sent, the BWOC's definition of apostle is purely functional and is just for the strategy of ministry. In other words, for them, an "apostle" is important only as far as starting churches, making disciples, and multiplying churches, are concerned and no more. What Broocks says about being an apostle is limited to being an evangelist. Instead of allowing various spiritual gifts to bear on his ministry, he draws resources almost exclusively from being an evangelist to plant and build new churches and to disciple them. Thus, his apostleship is manifested in the areas of evangelism and church planting, and other gifts are not empowered or released in his local leadership team. In this implementation of the apostolic, the governmental foundation is not established. There are no five-fold offices, nor is there an effort to establish such offices. I will discuss this area further in the next section in detail.

Definition of the Apostolic Role from Broocks and BWOC Congregation

According to Broocks, the primary role of an apostle is to reach out to the city and to preach the gospel of Christ.

> I mean, we have a job to do and that is to reach out [to the] city and so the people [can] hear. The apostolic role I see them (apostles) doing is to start things and get the ministry going and to preach the simple gospel of Christ. I don't think that I am as concerned about the theology of an apostle as I am [with] the work of the apostle. Whether you call me Pastor or Apostle Rice, I don't really think the average Bethel person would say "he is an apostle."

His strong emphasis lies on the evangelistic role of the apostle. However, his pastoral members' description of the role of an apostle differs from Broocks's. They describe the role of an apostle: "The role of an apostle is being a discipler, delegator, overseer, church planter." One of pastoral leadership mentioned the role of the apostle as "visionary leadership." Also, others express the role of an apostle as a pioneer who breaks ground. Many of the leaders recognized Ephesians 4:11–13, as they see the role of the apostle is to equip the saints along with prophets, pastors, teachers, and evangelists.

Additionally, pastoral leadership added "increase faith" as one of the roles of an apostle. One of them testifies how Broocks helped him to increase his faith and kept pushing him to the next level of having faith. This goes along with Broocks's understanding of the role of an apostle which can be described as a "discipler." One of the leaders strongly agreed with Broocks's understanding:

> The apostolic gifting is to set things in order and to set people in order. Pastor Rice has the gifting and anointing to set people in order. I love that he is mature as a leader. He hears from God to raise up leaders through discipleship.

The interview data from Broocks and the BWOC congregation agree with (19) carrying out the Great Commission; (24) church planting; and (27) one who lays a foundation as seen in Table 1. In terms of (19) carrying out the Great Commission, the role of apostle is manifested as a discipler.

The data from the BWOC shows a lack of "build-up" of the church aspect of the apostolic role. The strongest point of the role of the apostle, based on data from the BWOC, is planting churches and making disciples. In short, the role of apostle is to plant churches and to make disciples.

Even though their understanding of the apostolic role shows some weakness in the area of building up the church, data from Broocks and the BWOC congregation do measure up to Wagner's understanding of the apostolic role. Wagner insists the ideal role of apostle is to be a pioneer who goes into a territory first to found a church.[2] Broocks also agrees with Wagner's understanding of the apostolic role in terms of overseeing churches.[3]

Understanding of Apostolic-Concept from Broocks and BWOC Congregation

The main apostolic-concept from Broocks and the BWOC can be summarized into three areas: maximize-reach mindset, receiving prophetic words, and receiving healing power.

Maximize-Reach Mindset

Broocks teaches on maximize-reach mindset at the pastoral school. He calls it "How to Think Like an Apostle." He teaches on forty traits of how the apostle Paul thought. He explains how to distinguish an apostolic mindset from others by demonstration:

> Let me give you an example. When I talk to people on how to think like an apostle, it's like this. If I say to you, "Would you hand me that water I can't reach," and you're not really trying. An apostolic mindset is "Let's see how far I can reach. I am going to do everything I can to maximize our reach." Versus this "I can't do that." No, you're not even trying. You look at the apostle Paul. He was doing everything he could to maximize his reach. When we went to New York, I didn't think we could reach that far, but when I stretched I found out we could. So how far can you reach. What can you do? Most people don't even try, and they conclude they can't.[4]

---

2. Wagner, *Churchquake*, 107.
3. Wagner, *Churchquake*, 107.
4. Broocks, personal interview with author, October 5, 2007.

One of the pastoral leadership echoes Broocks "maximize-reach mindset" saying, "apostolic is the vision of going out and making a difference to places."

Receiving Prophetic Word

In terms of understanding the apostolic gift, the BWOC members speak of the prophetic vocation of apostle often. They mention how they received a prophetic word from the apostolic leaders as "God really spoke to my heart," "God speaking to me through a prophetic word," and "God touched me with prophetic word." Here is one of their testimonies:

> I'm sure you know Pastor Jim. He actually called my wife and I up out of the service. I had never met him before and he began to prophesy over us and spoke some things about our future. One of the things he said to me, the first time I had ever seen him, he looked at me in the face and said "a call on your life is in the full-time ministry. You will pastor a church one day." He began to give a little more detail on that. So I received that in 2001, and it wasn't until—well, I continued for the next five years to work in a pharmacy. And I saw that come to pass two and a half years [ago] when I was offered, and called on, to resign out of my pharmacy and come on full time staff here.

Receiving prophetic words is a big part of their Christian life and to discern God's heart as well. When they seek God in prayer, they expect to hear God's voice in their heart. One of the leaders expresses the nature of the prophetic word:

> I believe it was an impression. It was the Lord, the Holy Spirit, drawing me there [to understand prophetic word]. It also involved discernment. Rice asked me and I knew it was from the Lord. We never wanted to move here to the states. Never say Never. We had the direct leading and guiding from the Holy Spirit. I have had prophecy and words that have given me direction. It takes wisdom and insight from the Holy Spirit to exercise proper administration.

Receiving Healing

The last significant apostolic-concept from the BWOC is to receive healing power. The pastoral leaders express: "In BWOC, the gifts of the Spirit and

Case Study Three: Bethel World Outreach Center

healing are in operation here." Here are two testimonies by a pastoral leader on how he received healing power:

> My wife, last year or year and a half ago, was having severe heart problems. She went in for all sorts of tests. They had done all the major tests on her and found a major blockage there. . . . And when they did the last test on her that showed the blockage, he came in and said we are going to have to do surgery because there is a blockage in your heart. My wife did not want to do it because her father had five open heart surgeries in his lifetime, from the time he was 31–32 years old, so she watched him go through this, and just did not want to go through it. She said "I'm just nervous about it. I'm just going to believe God to heal me." And of course the doctor said, "You know we're not going to force you to have this surgery but I feel like you need to do this." So we talked her into doing it but we prayed for that day in the hospital and so basically after we prayed for her, they ran more tests the next day. The doctor came and got me out of the waiting room, brought me in back there and said: "I want you to look at this, we got a miracle."

> [There was a] man who [is a member] in our church who was in a tragic car wreck and his spinal cord was damaged. He had no movement, he was paralyzed. God healed him and he is in the process of healing. He was here on Sunday again and he is walking around on this walker.

The leaders of the BWOC and satellite churches are not afraid of exercising the gifts of healing. By presenting the testimony of healing experiences during the service, the leadership of the BWOC and the satellite churches encourage their congregations to believe and to practice healing prayer. One leader shared a concept of "thirty mighty men" as a prayer team believing in healing prayer:

> We have an interesting ministry here called our "thirty mighty men." They have this in Brentwood. Brentwood actually started this; I think it's a great ministry. It talks about if you remember in the life of David, he had thirty mighty men who worked with him. So we have what we call our "thirty mighty men," and anytime that there is a request for a prayer need out of this church or the Brentwood Church, we e-mail, and they e-mail our thirty mighty men and they (pray for the prayer request).

The data from Broocks and the BWOC agree with Table 1, (30) prophetic vocation; and (31) one who perform "signs, wonders, and miracles only for the divine confirmation of the gospel" in the biblical understanding of the apostolic-concept. The pastoral leadership receives prophetic words as a divine direction for their lives and expects to pray a healing prayer when they face the sick. These factors confirm the prophetic vocation of the apostolic-concept.

The contrast between biblical perspective and the BWOC's understanding can be found in (32) a spiritual gift for the church; and (33) a tool to equip the church. Because the BWOC sees Broocks as a strong apostolic leader, their understanding for apostle is a spiritual gift for the individual rather than a gift for the church. It suggests that the BWOC considers Broocks as a charismatic apostolic-evangelist who has a call to be an apostle. This goes with (33) a tool to equip the church viewpoint. Because they do not regard the apostolic gift for the church, they lack the sense of apostolic gift to equip the church. Compared to the role of apostle as a church planter and an evangelist, the BWOC shows a weakness in understanding apostolic gifts to equip the saints. As demonstrated above in the testimony section, one of the pastoral leaders strongly insists that Broocks's apostolic gifts are not for the congregation.

The BWOC's understanding of apostolic-concept goes with Wagner's concept that apostolic authority is the highest grid of authority.[5] They also agree with the fact that apostolic authority can be validated by ministry fruits, such as planting churches, doing evangelism, and healing the sick.[6] They openly called Broocks an apostolic-evangelist as Wagner has mentioned as an "hyphenated apostle."[7] The hyphenated apostle, such as apostolic-evangelist, is an apostle who performs more than one gift.[8]

Ecclesiology in the BWOC

In this section, based on the interviews with the local congregational members, I will review church planting as evangelism, city transformation as an apostolic mandate, and making disciples as an apostolic ministry. These three main factors will help to clarify the ecclesiology within the BWOC.

   5. Wagner, *Churchquake*, 105.
   6. Wagner, *Churchquake*, 115.
   7. Wagner, *Apostles and Prophets*, 52–53.
   8. Wagner, *Apostles and Prophets*, 52.

CASE STUDY THREE: BETHEL WORLD OUTREACH CENTER

Church Planting as Evangelism

Broocks believes that the most effective form of evangelism is planting a church. He consistently looks for an opportunity to plant a church throughout the Nashville area. The opportunity opens up sometimes by the Holy Spirit's leading, and other times by making an observation of possibilities. He testifies how he looks for an opportunity to plant a church:

> The key is just moving forward. Knocking on every door. So for me, as we spread out through this area, we knock on doors. We are looking for buildings, looking for opportunities. But there are certain things that are glaring, obvious things like downtown Nashville. Planet Hollywood is the closest. It's just like a beacon of light. It says go here. An evangelist went to Murfreesboro [satellite church] and leads a community, just like Philip who went down to Samaria in Acts chapter 8. He didn't get sent to Samaria. He went versus being sent. So he goes to Samaria and preaches, and there is such a revival. Then the apostles come down. That is how Murfreesboro got started. So now we are getting smarter as we are getting 6 more locations because people are coming to us from other parts of the city and we are finding out [what] their zip codes are. So we are seeing a whole groupings of people from one zip code or a different part of the city. It is a good indicator that there is something we need to look into in that area.

Broocks describes his church as missions-driven and culturally relevant apostolic ministry. Broocks focuses on planting churches as a means of training new leaders. The main goal of his ministry is to start a new church in a new location in surrounding cities and make disciples through the process of planting churches. The church understands the process of doing missions as reaching the city and changing the whole world. He expresses his strong sense to plant the church:

> For me, the challenge is how do I have five children, six locations, and still have a Call by the year 2020. I know I'm supposed to plant a church in every nation of the world, which is my call. It's just a question. Holy Spirit, how am I to keep the easy yoke on me which you promised. That's my ultimate challenge in life.

City Transformation as Apostolic Mandate

The second characteristic of apostolic ministry can be seen in the area of city transformation. Broocks insists that a local church has a mandate to reach the city. He quotes Matthew 28:18–20 as key verses.

> What I'm sensing is, the way it comes is, teaching the word and through releasing evangelists to a city. Not just to do crusades for Christians but to really penetrate a city. I've seen growth and I've seen new salvations happen here. So what I want to do is raise up a model that is a local church that reaches a city through primary evangelism.

The BWOC's catch phrase reflects city transformation as a mandate for the church, "reaching a city to touch the world."

Making Disciples as the Apostolic Mandate

To Broocks, making disciples is the first order of carrying out the apostolic mandate. He believes that making disciples should be the top burden for apostolic leadership. He sees his ability to focus on disciple-making as a cause for church growth:

> From January of 2000, we started to grow. The church really grew in attendance from 650 to a solid 2,800–2,900 within three years.... The growth? I think honestly that I am much more of a delegator, I think that he [the founding pastor] was much more of a teacher and things centered around his gift... discipling and empowering was the focus as well as diversity.

He continues to highlight the value of making disciple as a factor for church growth:

> I think Americans tend to look at the form and think that form is what is going to put them over. Just like they ran to Dr. Cho in the Eighties and thinking we're going to do what Dr. Cho did. They didn't get the church growth because they don't have his spirit and all the other things that are the real issues that put someone over. So I think that when we begin to value what Jesus values; disciple, true loving people, fathering, mothering, [then] the church will instantly grow.

Compare Biblical Ecclesiology and BWOC Ecclesiology

In comparing the BWOC's ecclesiology with Table 2, the BWOC agrees with numbers (5) participate in God's mission; (9) doing mission led by the Holy Spirit; and (16) sent out as a pioneer. The weaknesses observed when compared with the biblical understanding of church are in numbers (7) and (10), in the area of the intimate community that represents God's attributes in their everyday lives. Also, the data from BWOC disagree with (12) loving family without a hierarchical order. The BWOC pastoral structure portrays a high grid of hierarchical order with apostle Broocks on the top. Also lacking is (14) exercising gifts to hurdle the hierarchical concept of understanding and relating to each other. Even though strong gifts of apostleship are manifested in the BWOC, the rest of the congregation is not equipped to exercise their gifts in an everyday setting. This goes with (15) equipping saints using spiritual gifts which the data from BWOC disagrees with. The strength of BWOC's ecclesiology lies in planting churches and discipling people to plant churches rather than positioning the church to exercise their gifts and to equip their congregation to use their spiritual gifts to build the body of Christ.

New Characteristics of Apostolic Ministry in BWOC

In comparison to Wagner's ideal understanding of nine characteristics of the NARC, I identify two new characteristics of apostolic ministry reflected through the BWOC. This will help to determine the gap between the ideal and the reality as it pertains to BWOC in the context of the broader NARC movement.

First, spiritual anointing is the number one factor for selecting leadership position. Broocks explains how he selects his leadership members by sensing their anointing in their lives. This also means that Broocks himself uses his discerning gifts to sense others' anointing as a leader rather than considering their ministry experience, or educational background. In addition to his own discernment, he highly values the prophetic word that the prospective leader has received. Some of these prospective leaders often ask about a prophetic word that was spoken to them once in their lives to see if they have anointing and calling on their lives.

Secondly, a new characteristic from the BWOC is found in terms of reaching the city as a primary evangelistic tool. This means that in order to evangelize a city, they seek to have the church located in that particular city in their hands. Then, that local church has the responsibility to reach that particular city. Their understanding of evangelism is to reach the city through evangelism.

Determining the Gap between the Ideal and the Reality

In this section, I will analyze the data I just presented in order to identify the gaps between the ideal and the reality in the BWOC. In Table 9, I show a comparison of the BWOC's reality of the NARC with that of Wagner's ideal; and I will draw data from interviews of BWOC's congregational members and Broocks's apostolic team members.

Out of nine characteristics of NARC from Wagner's criteria, the data from the BWOC demonstrate five agreed, three disagreed, and one designated none of the above. In addition to the nine characteristics, BWOC shows two new characteristics of NARC related to the areas of reaching the city to touch the nations as primary evangelism and using discernment to fill prospective leadership positions. These two new characteristics reach beyond Wagner's nine characteristics.

Based on the review of Wagner's nine indicators of NARC, the strong agreements BWOC demonstrate are: (1) have a new name; (2) a new authority structure led by a "charismatic" pastor, (3) a new ministry focus, (4) a new outreach, and (5) new power priorities. The disagreements are in the areas of leadership training and lay ministries, worship style, and prayer styles. As Wagner states, the apostolic authority is validated by ministry fruits,[9] BWOC strives to do city outreaches by planting satellite churches to fulfill the apostolic mandate, under the new charismatic apostolic-evangelistic leadership with a vision for reaching the city to touch the nations. The model that BWOC portrays as a NARC is demonstrated in its strong sense of being sent to the city to carry out the mandate based on Matthew 28:18–20. They have a new name to signify what they believe they are, "Bethel World Outreach Center," rather than having a name with just "church." The outreach center is their picture for being church in their city.

---

9. Wagner, *Churchquake*, 115.

Table 9

The Gap between Ideal and Reality in Case Three

Wagner's Ideal Characteristics for a New Apostolic Ministry	BWOC's Reality Compared with Wagner's	
	Agreed or Disagreed with Wagner	New Characteristics
Having a "new" name to distinguish themselves from others	Agreed: Bethel World Outreach Center	N/A
New authority structure led by "charismatic" pastor-leaders who have a vision for what people can become	Agreed: Apostolic-evangelists as a senior pastor	N/A
Strong leadership training and lay ministries	Disagreed: Weak agreement of training leadership	N/A
New ministry focus	Agreed: Focus on the future rather than present	N/A
New worship style.	Disagreed: Traditional style	N/A
New prayer forms; earnest in prayer	Disagreed: Traditional style	N/A
New financing	N/A	N/A
New outreach; compassion for the lost; many ministries to the unchurched	Agreed: Planting church as a new form of outreach	Reach the city to touch the nations. Model as "a local church that reaches a city through primary evangelism."
New power priorities; passion for outpouring of God's Spirit.	Agreed: Focus on the prophetic word and healing power	Sense of anointing is the factor for selecting leadership position.

Although the BWOC shows strengths in doing evangelism to reach the city, the weakness was exposed in the area of "building church" by stimulating various spiritual gifts among the congregational life. Apostolic gift, evangelistic gift and prophetic gift, were identified among the apostolic leadership of the BWOC. However, the gift of pastor and teacher were not identified in either the leadership team or congregation.

The last remarkable factor from BWOC is their focus on new power priorities in the areas of receiving prophetic words, believing in healing power, and selecting leaders by spiritual anointing. Even though they did not show a contemporary worship style to host the Holy Spirit, they do invite the Holy Spirit in stimulating prophecy, healing and anointing. This happens not only at the apostolic leadership level, but also in congregational lives.

The gap between Wagner's ideal and the BWOC reality lies in three different areas: (1) strong leadership training and lay ministries; (2) new worship style; and (3) new prayer forms.

First Gap: Strong Leadership Training

The first gap between Wagner's ideal and BWOC's reality is in the area of training strong lay leadership. According to Wagner, NARC pastoral leadership is home grown without traditional seminary training.[10] In reality, BWOC selects their leadership based on a "sense of anointing" in their lives rather than home grown training. The present BWOC leadership asks the future leadership team member to participate in their own "Every Nation" training directly after the selection process. Once they select their leadership according to the anointing on their lives, the BWOC leadership begins to put them through "home grown" education regardless of their previous educational background. Therefore, this is a gap between Wagner's ideal and BWOC's real practice.

Second Gap: New Worship Style

The second gap between Wagner's ideal and BWOC's reality is in the area of having a new worship style. Wagner describes it as: "you will likely see some sitting, some kneeling, some looking at the ceiling, some lying prostrate on the floor, some holding up hands, some closing their eyes, some clapping their hands, some wiping tears from their eyes, some using tambourines, some dancing and some just walking around."[11] However, during

---

10. Wagner, *New Apostolic Reformation Church*, 21.
11. Wagner, *New Apostolic Reformation Church*, 22.

the worship service, BWOC shows none of the above, but are worshipping in a traditional style. For them, the contemporary worship style cannot definitely be an indicator of being a NARC.[12]

Third Gap: New Prayer Forms

The third gap shows in terms of new prayer forms. Compared to the traditional church, Wagner believes the worship service of the NARC excels in the amount of time spent on prayer.[13] Both the data from BWOC and my observation show there is no distinctive factor concerning prayer life. BWOC demonstrates it is similar to the traditional church style when they worship together.

To summarize the data from the three case churches, I present the findings in the next section where I compare and contrast the relation between the three case studies.

---

12. Wagner, *New Apostolic Reformation Church*, 22.
13. Wagner, *New Apostolic Reformation Church*, 23.

Chapter 8

Findings from Case Studies

THESE FINDINGS ADDRESS THE areas of the goals of the case studies and questionnaires of the case studies through, first, the apostleship and second, the ecclesial elements of NARC. Table 10 reports on apostleship for the case studies in three areas: definition, role, and concept. At the same time, the ecclesial elements of NARC are compared to Wagner's nine characteristics and Biblical Ecclesiology.

The goals of reporting the findings are to clarify a reality within NARC, and to identify the gap between the ideal and reality. The gap between ideal and reality will be reported in two areas; biblical and Wagner's theory. The structure of this report consists of describing evident indicators, identifying various indicators, identifying the nature of any gap, exposing any ineffectiveness for the twenty-first century NARC, and providing further recommendations.

Apostleship from Three Case Studies

For Fletcher in the first case study, an apostle is "a person who is gifted by God to equip the church with wisdom." In his view, apostleship has everything to do with strategy, growth, reaching one's community (their Jerusalem), planting churches, and reaching out in missions. An apostle is a gift given to the church for the building of a "healthy church" and fulfilling the Great Commission. Fletcher's manifestation of apostleship reflects Wagner's earlier understanding of leadership as being "flexible, coordinating, breaking boundaries, (and being) empowering."[1]

---

1. Wagner, *Apostles and Prophets*, 73.

Findings from Case Studies

Table 10

Indicators of Apostleship from the Case Studies

	Definition	Role	Concept
Case One	A person who is gifted by God to equip the church with wisdom	Build-up the local church	A tool to equip the church and incarnational humble servant.
Case Two	A person who provides an apostolic covering	An absolute authority in the local church and over the network of churches.	A tool to equip the church (highly limited to his family circle)
Case Three	A person who is sent for planting churches and strengthening the existing churches	Starting churches, and multiplying churches	A spiritual gift for the church (highly exclusive to the evangelistic area)

After analyzing the data from the unstructured interviews, I found that Fletcher, an apostle at Manna Church, did not confirm the biblical perspective on apostleship. However, in the process of analyzing data in light of biblical perspective and the NARC's own perspective, I find that apostle Fletcher confirms the biblical sense of apostleship in the areas of (25) building up the church; and (33) being a tool to equip the church, from Table 1. However, his apostleship fails to agree with the biblical usage of being a pioneer, a missionary, or in church planting. This suggests that his role of being an apostle is in building up a healthy local church as a senior pastor rather than in pioneering a church as an itinerant missionary. His strength as a builder for a strong local church is manifested in planting a multi-site campus in his city.

Similarly, Fletcher's concept of an apostle equipping the church is observed as equipping local congregational members to be strong and devoted church members in a local church rather than equipping people according to their own spiritual gifts to prepare for the work of ministry. Fletcher equips the congregational members to be cell leaders by stimulating their own lifestyle with activities such as hobbies, talents, and special skills. These unique lifestyles can be described as culturally familiar factors encouraging people to join the cell groups. The biblical term for equipping saints strictly means that gifted leaders help prepare people to stimulate their spiritual gifts. While stimulating their spiritual gifts, in the biblical perspective, the saints learn to be mature in Christ attaining to his full measure. Fletcher, in this sense, fails to equip people for works of service.

According to Mullen in the second case study, apostleship is heavily focused on "apostolic covering." In his view, an apostle has the highest office, position, or title, and also has absolute authority in the local church and over the network of churches. While an apostle is understood as a title and functions in the congregation, there are no other functioning offices from Ephesians 4:11. There is the recognition of the five-fold ministries, but in practice, only the position of the apostle is adapted and brought into existence to support a hierarchical, top-down leadership structure. Thus, he does not confirm the biblical sense of apostleship in terms of (26) and (27) from Table 1. The apostle is understood among his congregation as an absolute authority without proper accountability. While structurally, the board is above an apostle in his church, this is seen as a structural flow that hinders the effectiveness of the ministry. By this, Mullen has appropriated the authority of the office of an apostle without establishing the whole of the five-fold ministry.

In regard to the role and concept of apostleship in Mullen's view, there is a strong sense of equipping and releasing leaders. Unfortunately, the downside of his practice of equipping and releasing leaders is limited to his direct family members and relatives for the leadership circle. Thus, in this sense, his apostolic role and concept cannot be evaluated as being a biblical perspective on equipping all the saints.

For Broocks in case study three, an apostle is a person who is "sent for planting churches and strengthening the existing churches." To his congregation, an "apostle" is purely functional for the strategy of ministry; important only as far as starting and multiplying churches and no more. One of his leadership team members describes an apostle as being limited to being an evangelist. Instead of allowing various spiritual gifts to bear on his ministry, he draws resources almost exclusively from evangelists to plant and build new churches and to disciple them. Strictly speaking, the concept of being an apostle manifests in the area of evangelism and church planting; however, other gifts are not empowered or released in his congregation. The evangelist who plants a church becomes the head congregation-pastor of that church, who operates under Broocks, whom they recognize as their apostle.

To evaluate Broocks's apostleship, his evangelistic-apostolic gift manifests in the tension between his natural gift as a pioneer and his practical role as senior pastor over his local church. Because most of his congregation did not grasp the concept of the biblical sense of being an apostle as "sent one," his everyday role requires him to be a senior pastor who needs to maintain the organization of the church rather than pioneering and empowering the church. The lack of biblical understanding of building a church as being apostolic hinders Broocks's natural gift as evangelistic-apostolic from being fully released.

In summary, Fletcher's understanding and his implementation of the apostolic are gift oriented, but it is limited to the establishment of an apostle, without the four other gifts being established. It appears that this ministry has adopted the 1999 Wagner definition of "apostle." Mullen progressed forward to the 2002 definition of "apostle," but limited its application to the apostle and prophet, which happens to be the same person. The apostle is about the expansion of the church, whereby the new church plants become part of the one large church. Broocks's church also has limited application of the apostolic—to an apostle being a strategic tool that serves evangelism. The apostolic has to do with the apostle sending out evangelists (in which case the evangelist functions as an apostle) to plant churches.

The findings of apostolic leadership from the three case studies show the common missing factor of being a "sent one." The biblical apostle is a traveling missionary sent out for pioneering churches where there is none. The present stake of NARC's apostle, based on findings, struggle with the tension between "established boundaries of the local church" and "exercising apostolic leadership" in their present post-modern Christian context.

Ecclesial NARC Indicators Evident in Each Case Study

In this section, I will summarize the findings from the three case churches related to their ecclesial indicators. The findings will be compared with Wagner's NARC indicators to clarify the gap between the ideal of Wagner's theory and the reality from the data.

Ecclesial Indicators from Three Case Churches

I came to these decisions by selecting relevant words, phrases, and sentences from the interview transcript as they pertain to Wagner's indicators. These became evident when the interviewees described how they experienced the apostolic authority and apostolic ministry. As indicated in the focus on apostolic definition, role, and concept, I used these understandings of apostleship to arrive at these findings. The following is a brief explanation of Table 11, focusing on the most important indicators of each church:

Based on the review of the nine indicators of NARC, the strengths that partially fulfill the indicators for Manna Church, Fayetteville, North Carolina, are in its new leadership training and new ministry focus. Michael Fletcher, the senior pastor, and apostle of Manna Church, believes that the most important job for him is to set a strategy and help others discover their vision by motivating, inspiring, and depositing faith in them. This can be seen in his extensive leadership training program offered through his local church leadership and also in his network system called Grace Church International (GCI).

Fletcher's main focus for leadership training is to cast vision, raise faith, discover destiny, and understand the meaning of grace. According to Fletcher, the growth factors of the Apostolic Church were understood as spreading the Kingdom of God, understanding of destiny, creating grace, and being an outreach culture. Thus, his ministry focus is, through his teaching and training, to impart to leaders the understanding, inspiration, and increased faith to achieve these growth factors.

In a practical way, Fletcher's team claims that they are workers of the Kingdom of God, not just employees of the local church. That environment is thought to provide a safe place for the members to make trial and error in various areas including being a cell leader, being a volunteer, and being an intercessor. While it may be easier for the outsiders (non-church members) to recognize the correlation between their emphasis on grace and his apostolic leadership, the average church members are not aware of the term, "apostolic."

Mullen, from Word of Life Church, agrees that the main force of an apostolic ministry is the Holy Spirit. They stress the "passion for the outpouring of the Holy Spirit" often in terms of praying, worshipping, and doing missions. Mullen claims that he seeks the Holy Spirit's counsel whenever he needs a new direction for the ministry. His team also strongly believes that the mark of apostolic ministry is to recognize the Holy Spirit's presence and an outpouring of the Holy Spirit in people's hearts. His church recognizes Mullen as an apostle by his leadership over an apostle's coalition and for his prophetic gift, accompanied by signs, wonders, and miracles. Mullen insists that the strong authority of an apostolic ministry is necessary for effective ministry today. He embodies an hierarchical form of leadership as an effective equipping tool for his congregation.

Findings from Case Studies

Table 11
Indicators of Ecclesiology from the Case Studies

NARC indicators from C. Peter Wagner	Case Study One: Manna, Fayetteville, NC (USA)/ Michael Fletcher	Case Study Two: Word of Life, Red Deer (Canada)/Mel and Heather Mullen	Case Study Three: Bethel World Outreach, Brentwood TN, (USA)/Rice Broocks
1) New name			Bethel World Outreach Center
2) New authority structure; led by "charismatic" pastor-leaders; vision for what people can come	Pastor of prayer and evangelism	Apostle for one church in many locations	Evangelistic apostle, however, the authority structure remains like a denominational church
3) New leadership training; strong lay ministries; every member and every seeker receives regular pastoral care from a layperson.	Kingdom focused Equip the saints	Gift based various ministry	"How to think like an apostle" - leadership training school. Strong evangelistic leadership training. Main leaders were evangelists
4) New ministry focus; small groups; family feeling, but not exclusive	Empowering gifts A cell church Focus on DNA	Relational based church	Small groups
5) New worship style.	Lifting their hands freely Contemporary worship		Contemporary
6) New prayer forms; earnest in prayer		Hearing prayer Making decisions based on prayer Invite the Holy Spirit while they prayed	
7) New financing			
8) New outreach; compassion for the lost; many ministries to the unchurched; obedience to the Great Commission; cultural adaptation to the target population	Strong outreach ministry Five to six church planting in the USA	Planting church as an outreach	Six different campuses. Planting churches is the main evangelistic outreach. Try to be relevant to the context of culture when they plant the church
9) New power priorities; passion for outpouring of God's Spirits.	Hosting God's presence	Fasting and praying for Holy Spirit leading	Prayer for the sick

Broocks describes his church as missions driven and a culturally relevant apostolic ministry. Broocks focuses on planting churches as a means of training new leaders. The main goal of his ministry is to start a new church in a new location in surrounding cities and make disciples through planting churches. Although the leadership over BWOC recognizes Broocks as an apostolic leader, signs, wonders, and miracles are not sought after in the congregation. The church understands doing missions as reaching the city and changing the whole world. Thus, their priority in missions lies in the local city, and not so much in doing outreach outside of the city. One of the outstanding atmospheres within BWOC is their harmony in ethnic diversity. Compassion for the lost and ministries to the unchurched were demonstrated in their adaptation of cultural relevancy to the target population.

Biblical Ecclesiology from Three Case Studies

In terms of biblical ecclesiology in Manna Church, the life of congregants confirms Table 2, (14) exercising gifts to hurdle the hierarchical concept of understanding and relating to each other; and (15) equipping saints by using spiritual gifts. This evidence can be observed in the areas of cell ministry.

Even though Fletcher contends that his gifts equip him to be an apostolic-teacher, the structure of Manna Church disagrees with his apostolic function. There is an apostolic-teacher, but there are no indicators of prophet, evangelist, and pastoral leader. Fletcher identifies the growth factors for the church as the degree of awareness in the sense of calling and destiny, awareness of Kingdom perspective, grace, and creating an outreach culture. These particular factors parallel with building a strong local church, rather than being a "sent one" to the community as in a Missional Church. Thus, the missional and apostolic aspects of Manna Church fail in terms of being "sent" to the community and demonstrating pioneering spirit as a Missional Church.

Part of the manifestations of Mullen's ministry is the fact that he has implemented the "empowering" aspect of Wagner's earlier gift-oriented definition of apostle.[2] But the majority (80 percent) of those who are empowered by the apostle, that is Mullen, as next generation leaders are his male, extended family members. Empowerment, thus, happens in a safe environment, rather than in an open environment. In an open environment,

---

2. Wagner, *Churchquake*, 73.

any gifted person is identified, trained, and released to be a leader according to God-given gifts. Thus Mullen's practice of empowering would represent a departure from Wagner's 2002 description of apostle as one who would "establish the foundational government of the church within an assigned sphere of ministry,"[3] since those that are established are largely his family members, and the establishment does not reflect the five-fold ministry.

One of the pastoral leaders from Broocks's church, states that an apostle is a "sent one," who has evangelistic gifts and whose job is to extend the church borders into new areas where the Gospel has not been preached. The planted churches are referred to as satellite campuses and are part of BWOC. As far as he observes from his ten years at BWOC, the apostolic has nothing to do with the life of a congregation, since the apostolic ministry is limited to evangelism and satellite church planting. In this implementation of the apostolic, the governmental foundation is not established. There are no five-fold officers, nor is there an effort to establish such offices.

Nature of the Gap between the NARC Ideal and Reality

The nature of the gap between the NARC ideal and the reality of the NARC can be found in the areas of adaptation issues where reality went beyond theory and the maturing process.

Adaptation Issues

Based on the literature of the NARC, *apostolus* means a sent one; "as the father has sent me, so I send you."[4] However, since the meaning of apostle should be focused on mission, the reality of *apostolus* is now the leadership of the church. It means that in the Apostolic Churches concerned about leadership of the church, *apostolus* is no longer missional, but an institutional leadership figure.

Reality Went Beyond the Theory

In reality, the main focus of NARC's ministry, according to these three case studies, is to build a healthy, biblical church. To build a healthy church is more important than equipping saints. In this case, the reality went beyond

---

3. Wagner, *Spheres of Authority*, 27.
4. Cannistraci, *Apostles*, 72.

their own theory—equipping saints is the main focus of NARC—in order to carry their evangelistic mission into their ministry, whatever that may be.[5]

Maturing Process

Following the birth of the NARC Movement in the early 1990s, there was a remarkable phenomenon taking place in North America, the birth of prophetic prayer and an awareness of prophetic gifts in the body of Christ. Once prophetic prayer and prophetic gifts were released in the Movement, which took about ten years, the position of Apostle came forth in the body of Christ. When apostles were identified, teachers, pastors, and evangelists began to emerge. I believe that these issues illustrate the phrase in Ephesians 4:13; "become mature, attaining to the whole measure of the fullness of Christ."

Effectiveness of the Twenty-First-Century Apostolic Church

The gap between theory and practice in the NARC impedes the effectiveness of their mission in the body of Christ. For example, the most outstanding gap comes from the governing structure of the NARC; a five-fold ministry (Eph 4:11). The discussion on this "five-fold ministry" is placed in the middle of its theory. However, the reality of the NARC is to highlight the ministry of the apostle, not the ministry of the saints or the equipping of the saints.

Ephesians 4:11–13 has been the NARC's key passage, highlighting the need to equip the saints for the work of the ministry. In theory, the main job of the senior pastor of a NARC, who is also called the Apostle, is to equip the congregation to do the ministry. This is in contrast to the modern church's conception that the senior pastor preoccupies himself with preaching, pastoral counseling, visiting the ill, and so on.

In the ideal concept of the NARC, an apostolic ministry does not exist in order to preserve or maintain the institution itself. Rather, it functions around a structured and linear form of ministry in order to be effective in service. Despite the attempt to avoid church bureaucracy, the structure of the NARC remains hierarchical. According to Mullen of WOLC, the

---

5. Wagner, *Changing Church*, 119.

strong authority of a new Apostle is necessary for effective ministry today. He embodies a hierarchical form of leadership as an effective tool for equipping his congregation.

In the New Apostolic Reformation Movement, being an Apostolic Church means being a part of God's apostolic mission. As John 15 states, "You have not chosen me, but I have chosen you, and I appointed you" (John 15:16). The biblical understanding of apostolic ministry is being sent out to the world to make disciples for the kingdom of God, with emphasis on who is particularly being sent. When the present NARC begins to explore its own reality in light of biblical perspective, the church will begin to be a "being-sent-out" people into the world. This will then become their main contribution to the body of Christ.

Summary

In general, my data shows that the three cases studies of NARCs do not measure up to Wagner's criteria. The first issue seems to arise from the fact that the definition of "apostle" went through a process of development. The limitations in implementing Wagner's 2002 definition of "apostle" seem to arise from developmental stages. The definition of "apostle" went through a series of stages, opening up doors for different levels of implementation by various leaders either according to one's theological understanding of the biblical texts or according to one's exposure, preference, or circumstances.

In terms of apostolic ministry, based on the analysis of the data, my initial observation is that the most outstanding gap comes from the governing structure of the NARC. Based on Ephesians 4:11–13, the apostolic government consists of what is considered a "five-fold ministry:" apostle, prophet, teacher, pastor, and evangelists. The discussion on this "five-fold ministry" is placed in the middle of its theory. However, the ministry around the "five-fold," concept indeed creates the greatest gap between theory and practice when the biblical text is being examined.

The critical reason why there is an outstanding gap between ideal and reality within the present NARC is that there is not enough clarity provided by Wagner and others on what an apostle is and what the apostolic foundational government should look like. The description of the apostolic foundational government stops with the promotion of it. It fails to explain in detail how the apostolic ministry with its five-fold ministry and officers should be established and how that five-fold ministry and those who carry out these offices ought to function to equip the saints in the five-fold gifts.

For this reason, there is considerable variation among my three case studies as it relates to what an apostle is and how each function within the context of each church as well as within the network of churches around the world.

In addition to the lack of biblical guidance to be apostolic, the limitation that the NARC has in implementation lies in the absence of clear directives. Notice that in all the three cases, the apostleship is affirmed and elevated in the near absence of other gifts or offices. It is very evident that in order for an apostle to be an apostle in an apostolic ministry, this leader needs to be equipped to work with other officers. If the presence of an apostle is crucial for the success of the apostolic ministry, then it would be equally true that prophets, teachers, evangelists, and pastors also need to be identified as complements in an apostolic ministry setting in accordance with Ephesians 4:11–12.

The following are concluding points based on the case studies from the NARC which I hope will make a significant contribution in closing the gap.

1. Each apostle is unique in the realization of their gifts—Apostolic teachers, Apostolic evangelists, and Apostolic prophets. Apostolic leaders need to discover their own gifts in order to lead the church in a unique way.
2. The spiritual DNA of the new apostolic ministry is manifested in the area of understanding destiny. Individual destiny is connected to corporate destiny, meaning that the destiny of individual believers is related to the church destiny. Therefore, it is crucial for leaders to understand their own gifts and destiny for the congregation in order that the members of the congregation can enter their own destiny.
3. Apostles have their own spheres. Not every apostle functions the same way. Therefore, it is important to discover their gifts, which in turn will impact their sphere of influence and then determine effectiveness based on how they exercise their gifts.
4. Hearing from God is a mark of apostleship in order for them to build a church according to his expectations. Hearing from God is also a mark of apostleship that helps them to know their personal sphere of influence as well as how God wants them to reach the city.
5. The acts of "releasing," "being a coach-stay behind the game" and "exercising grace" are the ways of equipping saints.

6. Marks of church growth:
   - Understanding the Kingdom of God
   - Grace
   - Transforming the city, or reaching the nations
7. Marks of apostles:
   - Not by signs, wonders, miracles, but by character
   - Releasing the next generation of leaders
   - Has more than one function—apostolic teacher, apostolic prophet
   - Has unique spheres in their spiritual authority
   - Hearing from God through fasting and prayer
   - Stay behind the game as equipping the saints

The maturing process of the NARC will continue in terms of forming ecclesiology, clarifying the meaning of mission in contemporary culture, and bringing authentic manifestations of Christianity to the body of Christ. In Part III, I move toward the twenty-first-century biblical apostle and biblical apostolic ministry in light of two other missiological movements in North America: the emerging and missional movements.

Part III

Moving toward a Biblical Church in North American Context with a Broader Perspective

In the light of a comprehensive biblical exegesis of certain Bible passages, Part II identified the need for the NARC to pay attention to biblical ecclesial elements which they have missed. In this section, I provide a survey of the broader picture in the context of the North American church in relation to church growth issues, Missional Church, and the Emerging Church. This survey of the broader ecclesial context in the contemporary North American context will play a critical role in envisioning a biblical church in the twenty-first century in North America.

Chapter 9

Ecclesial Elements and Church Growth in North America

BASED ON THE FINDINGS of Part II, the New Apostolic Reformation Church is a manifestation of the charismatic church in a contemporary context. Similarly, Emerging Church is a manifestation of evangelical churches in a contemporary context, and Missional Church is a manifestation of denominational churches in a contemporary context. The New Apostolic Reformation Church contains both the contributions toward a biblical church in the twenty-first century and the overlooked biblical and ecclesial elements. In order for the New Apostolic Reformation Church to envision a biblical ecclesiology, it is crucial to consider the contributions of other movements; the Emerging Church and the Missional Church in the light of the twenty-first-century North American contemporary context.

The primary contribution of the NARC in the area of envisioning a biblical church is to bring a sending-concept back to ecclesiology. When we look back on previous centuries of ecclesiology, both missiology and ecclesiology have separated disastrously. As the NARC strives to reinstate the concept of apostle, the church will begin to gear itself towards a missional direction. The biblical role of the apostle is to make the church missional by emphasizing a sending-concept. Although the current NARC has failed to demonstrate the biblical role of apostle, its contribution in reinstating the role of apostle is evident. If the current NARC is schooled on being a biblical church, its potential contribution toward a biblical ecclesiology will be enhanced.

For this very reason, I take a closer look at the fruits and potential contributions of Emerging and Missional Churches in this section. The intention of considering the fruits of Emerging and Missional Churches is to encourage a greater awareness of a biblical aspect within the NARC. I am urging the current NARC to learn from Emerging and Missional Churches so that it can be positioned to be a more biblical church. I present the fruits of Emerging and Missional Churches as criteria for the NARC to critique itself. Reflecting on the Emerging and Missional Church will strengthen the ability of the NARC to be biblically apostolic in the contemporary North American context.

Therefore, in this chapter, I discuss ecclesial elements that are church governing facets within two divisions: (1) What really makes the church to be biblical, and (2) what the ministry, structure, and sacraments of the church are based on, in light of the discussions of current missiologists and theologians of North America. This will help to highlight the critical essence of defining the biblical church. I pay special attention to the critical essence which enables the church to be a biblical church.

Ecclesial Elements in the North American Church

The current discussion around the ecclesial elements can be observed in two divisions: what defines the church and what ought to form the church's ministry? Drawing inspiration from theologian Veli-Matti Kärkkäinen, the principle of how Christology has been divided can be easily applied to the discussion of the ecclesial elements by asking two important questions; "What makes the church, in fact, the church?" and "What should form the ministry, structure, and sacraments of the church?" His insight sprang out of observing the persona and the work of Christ in Christology, "Christology has been divided into two parts, namely the persona and the work of Christ: who Christ is, and the derivative topics."[1] Although Kärkkäinen fails to show how the two relate to each other, his consideration of breaking down ecclesiology into two divisions has advanced the discussion around ecclesial elements in terms of distinguishing the nature and the work of the church.

To take his insight in Christology a step further, if the question of who Christ is bears importance on atonement and faith, then the same principle should apply to ecclesiology. In other words, the ministry, the structure and the sacraments of the church will rely heavily on the perspective of

---

1. Kärkkäinen, *Introduction to Ecclesiology*, 14.

what makes the church the church. The conditions for being a church will determine the shape of the church's overall ministry.

Borrowing Dan Kimball's criteria for measuring the success of the church applies to Kärkkäinen's idea of Emerging ecclesiology. Kimball states:

> The Emerging Church must redefine how we measure success: by the characteristics of a kingdom-minded *disciple of Jesus* produced by the Spirit, rather than by our methodologies, numbers, strategies, or the cool and innovative things we are *doing*.[2]

Kimball's concern is not just helpful for forming what he calls an "Emerging ecclesiology," but it can be largely applied to the current field of ecclesiology in North America. Though he did not directly mention the relationship between being and doing, Kimball implies that what we do as the church cannot take precedence over who we are as the body of Christ.

Echoing Kimball, Ray Anderson also highlights that the measurement of the Emerging Church desperately needs an appropriate way to form ecclesiology.[3] According to Anderson, a Kingdom-minded disciple is a new kind of Christian in what he identifies as Kimball's passion produced by the Spirit rather than by methodologies, numbers, strategies, the cool and innovative things.[4]

On the other hand, Charles Van Engen wisely warns against the critical impact of modern ecclesiology on the local church.[5] Van Engen's method is different from both Kimball's and Anderson's, because he considers how missiology has erred by observing the historical impact of modern ecclesiology. Specifically, he summarizes how modernity has reshaped the missiology of theologians like Dietrich Bonhoeffer, Johannes Gustave Warneck, and W. Douglas Smith.[6]

Van Engen assists readers by pointing them to Smith's writings when he says: "The historical expansion of the church could be described as the missionary people of God striving to emerge, not only numerically, culturally, and geographically, but also spiritually, structurally, organizationally, theologically, architecturally, musically, and economically."[7] Although I

---

2. Kimball, *Emerging Church*, 15.
3. Anderson, *Emergent Theology for Emerging Churches*, 8.
4. Anderson, *Emergent Theology for Emerging Churches*, 13.
5. Van Engen, *God's Missionary People*, 37.
6. Van Engen, *God's Missionary People*, 35–43.
7. Van Engen, *God's Missionary People*, 42.

question Smith's placement of the spiritual alongside the organizational aspects of the church, I am thrilled to see his distinction between the spiritual and the numerical parts of the church. The "new paradigm" of missional ecclesiology is a process relating to what the church is and what it becomes.[8] Reshaping ecclesiology opens the window for the interaction between missiology and ecclesiology.

If it is true that modern ecclesiology has shifted to a new paradigm, and the need to reconsider how the church ought to look at its mission in the past, then it is crucial to reflect on the interaction between the two divisions: what makes the church the church, and the ministry, structure, and sacraments of the church.

The Criteria for Church Growth in North America

In an attempt to consider what makes the church the church, and the ministry, structure, and sacraments of the church, it is important to look at church growth theory and its impact on modern ecclesiology.

McGavran and Numerical Growth

Throughout the 1970s and 1980s, Donald McGavran laid the foundations of church growth. Ryan Bolger explains in his recent article how McGavran's influence has diminished as interest in church growth waned in the late 1980s: "Church growth was criticized at several points: reliance on segregated homogenous units, separation of conversion from spiritual formation, and reliance on numerical growth as primary criterion of growth."[9]

Is church growth no more than a sociological process?[10] Does the numerical approach McGavran employs really help us to understand biblical church growth?[11] Clearly the missiologists of the 1960s and 1970s who comprised the pioneering group and discerned the factors of church growth in North America understood church growth from a behavioral science perspective rather than biblical perspective. Although I agree with McGavran about the value of the numerical approach in human endeavors

---

8. Van Engen, *God's Missionary People*, 41.
9. Bolger, "Practice Movements," 182.
10. McGavran, *Understanding Church Growth*, 7.
11. McGavran, *Understanding Church Growth*, 67.

like industry, commerce, finance, research, government, and inventions,[12] I believe that there is room for further discussion about utilizing numbers for understanding biblical church growth. Understanding how perspectives on biblical church growth emerged is helpful in understanding how church growth has become such an important criterion in forming ecclesiology in North America.

Will church growth continue to be measured primarily by numerical growth? Will Christians in the Emerging Churches and Missional Churches agree with McGavran's perspective? Douglas John Hall, a contextual theologian, provides helpful insight in understanding the dangers of McGavran's numerical approach. He discusses how the Christian "Diaspora" in North America (relating the denominational crisis to the Diaspora in Acts) can be the solution to the crisis of mainline Protestantism.[13] He connects the excessive emphasis on numbers to this crisis when he passionately poses the question:

> Will the hunger for numbers and finances drive the churches to adopt yet more desperate, market-oriented, gauche, and "gimmicky" programs of church growth, "packaging" the "gospel-product" in increasingly sloganized and unthinking ways that will alienate thoughtful people even more conspicuously than at present?[14]

Hall's call for the disestablishment of mainline Protestantism is an important one. With the emphasis away from church numbers, things like divine grace, justifying faith and obedience to Jesus as the Christ can assume priority in asking our initial question, "What makes the church the church?"[15] He goes on to discuss the prophets' ability to take their cues from being led by the Holy Spirit. Such sensitivity to the Spirit allows them the ability to discern God's movement in the cultural context and requires a lot of boldness from them. As Hall continues, "They [the prophets] dared to assume that they understood something of God's [intentions]."[16]

---

12. McGavran, *Understanding Church Growth*, 67.
13. Hall, *Confessing the Faith*, 256–64.
14. Hall, *Confessing the Faith*, 262.
15. Hall, *Confessing the Faith*, 263.
16. Hall, *Confessing the Faith*, 263.

Beyond Numerical Growth

While I draw inspiration from theologians who talk about the crisis in mainline Protestantism and question how church growth is measured by the numerical approach, I am not blaming any party or individual. Rather, I am probing others in order to discern for myself where the Holy Spirit is leading for the future direction of ecclesiology beyond numerical church growth. Only by engaging those outsides of particular movements can a "fuller" ecclesiology emerge.

Thus far, my probing has led me to process much more information than I initially anticipated. It is helpful to consider Kärkkäinen's comments upon the combined work of various ecclesiologists: "All of these theologians highlight the importance of the essence of the church before one talks about the ministry and functions of the church. The church first is the church, before it does the work of the church."[17] As one continues to consider the works of important ecclesiologists, one must pay particular attention to how these theologians and scholars highlight the 'essence' of the church, before moving toward discussions on the 'work' of the church. Kärkkäinen continues on to define the very 'essence' of the church as its foundational missionary nature, and not merely the ways in which a church engages in missions: "The church exists as a mission; mission belongs to the 'essence' of the community of God."[18] With this careful
distinction, I shift to consider other theologians' contributions.

In addition to Kärkkäinen, several other scholars have attempted to emphasize the importance of being Christians in their communities as salt and light, rather than elevating the importance of increasing the number of believers in a church. In order to gain a bearing on the shifts taking place within the Christian community in North America, I will focus on these theologians and beyond. Specifically, I will attempt to contrast their ecclesial form from modern ecclesiology, with particular attention to the importance of being a Christian over being sent.

Christianity and Church Growth in North America

If Christians in North America should move beyond pursuing numerical church growth, what exactly should they be moving toward? What other

---

17. Kärkkäinen, *Introduction to Ecclesiology*, 160.
18. Kärkkäinen, *Introduction to Ecclesiology*, 160.

biblical criteria are there for church growth? These are basic questions for consideration with which Christians in North America have wrestled and struggled.

Shifting from Numerical Approach

Ryan Bolger was correct when he observed that, in the 1990s, "the term 'church growth' lost much of its association with McGavran and became associated instead with church marketing and the growth of the suburban mega-churches."[19] As we have established, "church growth," according to McGavran, was based on his numerical approach. Lesslie Newbigin discusses McGavran's approach and notes that McGavran asked the right questions in relation to his own church context.[20] But his approach was in response to missionaries who were not actually producing new believers. He had criticized missions for placing demands for moral conformity at the center of the church, and not the liberating gospel.[21] Newbigin asserts that McGavran is right to press the question, "Why there isn't more concern for the multiplication of believers, and where is the evidence that the church is growing?"[22] Thus, his emphasis on increasing numbers was appropriate to that context; while perhaps now, in the post-modern context, other emphases are more appropriate.

While I am content with Newbigin's discussion on McGavran's position, I would like to analyze further to understand what Newbigin and others have to say about church growth, conversion, and culture.[23] This discussion will prepare me to gather the essence of biblical ecclesiology offered by two particular church movements in chapter 10.

Shifting to "Community of Spirit"

Out of the all theologians whose books I read, none suggested where or how to move forward from the numerical growth mentality. As I will expound later, each theologian periodically highlighted the importance, role of the Holy Spirit, and the importance of the fruit of the Holy Spirit as evidence

---

19. Bolger, "Practice Movements," 182.
20. Newbigin, *Open Secret*, 124–28.
21. Newbigin, *Open Secret*, 127.
22. Newbigin, *Open Secret*, 127.
23. Newbigin, *Open Secret*, 121–59.

of the church in ecclesiology. Whether or not these previous church growth specialists would articulate it this way, their attention to the work of the Holy Spirit supports my suggestion that the most helpful way of moving forward from McGavran's numerical approach is by shifting the focus to the works and growth of the inner maturity: fruit of the Spirit.[24]

Newbigin discusses the live experience of the Holy Spirit in the Christian community.[25] Newbigin's central placement of the Holy Spirit in the church is more developed and therefore especially helpful in his later works. Focusing attention on the live experience of the Spirit is to employ what he calls the "Pentecostal approach." This is one of the three ecclesiological streams he goes on to describe.[26] Later, he considers the Reformers' acknowledgment of the Holy Spirit's role in the church and introduces what he calls "the community of the Holy Spirit" to the discussion. He clearly connects the question, "Where is the church?" with the question, "Where is the power of the Holy Spirit recognizably present?"[27] Finally, Newbigin begins to form a modern missionary Ecclesiology based on these considerations.

Similarly, Roland Allen, a missionary from China during the early part of the twentieth century, expressed his understanding of the active work of the living Holy Spirit as the cause of the multiplication of believers in missions. He mentions twelve different instances in the book of Luke that demonstrate how the Holy Spirit is the leading force in missions. As he affirms, the Holy Spirit is also the cause and core of missions throughout the book of Acts.[28]

Later, Craig Van Gelder describes how the marks of the church emerged as the church was led and taught by the Spirit. This is to be a core part of the ministry of the church.[29] He also connects corporate community life to the life led by the Spirit. His Protestant confession includes "the church governs all its life by the Word as it is led and taught by the Spirit," and thus Van Gelder positions the Holy Spirit as an initiating force for the ministry of the church.[30]

---

24. For summary of Eph 4:11–13, see pages 21–29. [x-ref]
25. Newbigin, *Open Secret*, 151.
26. Newbigin, *Open Secret*, 153.
27. Newbigin, *Open Secret*, 156.
28. Allen, *Ministry of the Spirit*, 44–51.
29. Van Gelder, *Essence of the Church*, 142.
30. Van Gelder, *Essence of the Church*, 143.

In addition to Van Gelder, Newbigin, and Allen, Ray S. Anderson seeks the "community of the Spirit," and not just the "gifts of the Spirit," as one theological criterion for Emerging Churches today. He strongly insists that the purpose of an individual having spiritual gifts is for the community and not an honorary title for personal exaltation.[31] The gifts of the Spirit are often interpreted as the means by which church members are equipped to carry out their ministries. As part of the equipping process, members should take an inventory of what gifts may be sought or are currently in use[32]

Anderson continues that this kind of "shopping for gifts" is a way of mobilizing lay persons for ministry and has often produced a lot of initial enthusiasm and burst of energy within communities, but equally as often, it leads to both personal frustration and spiritual fatigue.[33] When this kind of abuse of spiritual gifts occurs, the church becomes just another marketplace that offers a product—in this case, spiritual gifts.

I affirm Anderson's sharp contrast between using spiritual gifts for the community and the abuse of spiritual gifts, in the above example of "shopping for gifts." To guard against such abuses, he warns that true empowerment "comes through the life of Christ that flows through us as the Holy Spirit touches the core of our own spirit."[34]

All of these church growth specialists uphold the importance of the Holy Spirit and the sound biblical use of spiritual gifts for biblical church growth. The point is that the Christian community cannot be formed without the Holy Spirit's leading—whether it is in the mission field or in your own neighborhood. Moreover, the gifts of the Spirit cannot properly function until we have formed an authentic and biblical Christian community from which believers can be empowered. Without the Holy Spirit's leading, then, we are left with only numerical growth as our sign of church growth.

Without the Holy Spirit's leading, how can we know that the community, congregation, and church are growing other than by means of counting converts? What is the relationship between forming biblical Christian communities and assessing biblical Christian growth? I will address all of these vital questions in the following section in order to reflect the biblical sense of church growth in the twenty-first-century North American context.

31. Anderson, *Emergent Theology for Emergent Churches*, 177.
32. Anderson, *Emergent Theology for Emergent Churches*, 158–77.
33. Anderson, *Emergent Theology for Emergent Churches*, 172.
34. Anderson, *Emergent Theology for Emergent Churches*, 172.

Holy Spirit's Community and Reality

Although none of the theologians or missiologists in the previous discussion suggest where or how to move forward from McGavran's and Wagner's numerical growth mentality, we can draw strong inferences from the early church for the merit of the work of the Holy Spirit in leading and creating newness among Christians. The early church experienced the rise of Christianity with phenomenal numerical growth through the acts of breaking bread together, sharing possessions, praising God, and through the receiving of the Holy Spirit. It means that the numerical growth from the early church was based on forming an authentic community. Furthermore, the fruit of the Holy Spirit enabled the early church to draw attention to nonbelievers. I will illustrate two brief interviews to address the reality of the modern church community and Christianity in the North American cultural context.

The Reality of Christian Community

During the summer of 2007, on the street in Durham, North Carolina, I spoke to thirty people about Jesus and the church. They were randomly selected from places in my neighborhood like Wal-Mart, K-Mart, the Dollar Store, Wendy's restaurant, the supermarket, the post office, and so on. None of them was a regular church-goer. However, 90 percent of them expressed belief in God and Jesus. As I talked to them, I remembered having read the surprising statistics that revealed a peculiar thing about North American Christianity: that North American Christians do not often connect church with God. I learned from the people I shared Christ with that they considered themselves believers even though they did not belong to a local church.

In the narrative interaction that follows, the effect on the modern church community and Christianity in the North American context was made obvious. I met with Arthur at the Dollar Store on Broad Avenue in Durham. He was cleaning the shelves when I got there. As I engaged in a conversation with him, I learned that he previously attended church as a young adult when he was twenty. Yet at this time, Arthur was aged 50, but he no longer attended church. I also learned that this man was once a preacher. He explained that the reason why he no longer attends church is because he does not believe that many church-goers are actually Christians. This belief emerged out of an estranging experience he had in the church twenty-five years ago. One day, Arthur came to church with his African-American friend. Though his friend was somehow officially welcomed by the congregation, yet it was clear that in their hearts, the people did not want him there. After the church service, a man walked up to Arthur and whispered: "Don't bring him again to my church." The man meant for Arthur to get out of there with that African-American fellow! Discouraged by this attitude, Arthur concluded that many church goers were not kind and did not know Jesus at all.

At another time, I met Betsy while I was walking near my apartment in Durham. She owned two dogs and asked if I would mind looking after them while she attended a funeral. Though she had lived in one location for eight or nine years, she did not regularly go to church. Betsy did not know anyone in whose care she could keep her dogs. Betsy's loneliness in her environment and inability to get somebody take care of her dogs clearly suggested the lack of a sense of Christian community in the North American church.

From the above two real life stories, it is obvious that the average North American Christian does not experience the biblical community fellowship that was a way of life for early church Christianity. Meanwhile, in the next section, I will discuss the nature of Christian community based on biblical inspiration.

Nature of Christian Community

Therefore, what are the marks of being an authentic Christian community? From the above two real life stories, this is apparently not an easy question to answer. Guder explains that "the understanding of the church which emerges is well summarized by the statement that the church's mission is not secondary to its *being*; the church exists in *being sent* and in building up itself for the sake of its being."[35]

Being Sent

The nature of being a Christian community is in the community's ability to share love, joy, peace, patience, kindness, goodness, faithfulness, gentleness and self-control (Gal 5:22–24) with others. In other words, the element of "being sent" which is the biblical way of being apostolic is the nature of the

---

35. Guder, *Missional Church*, 1–17.

Christian community. These apostolic elements are the marks of the early church and are the main reasons why people are attracted to a believers' community.

Rodney Stark provides the connection between the importance of community with the idea of church growth. Stark reports: "the basis for successful conversion movements is growth through social networks, through a structure of direct and intimate interpersonal attachments."[36] He explains that it is easier to find community in urban places because the environment allows for a walking-distance lifestyle and for "undisclosed" openness that fosters intimacy in Christian communities. Small, private spaces provide a social network system among urban Christians. The function of these urban communities as a social network is one crucial factor for the conversion of new believers.

Stark goes on to explain that as they share small spaces with each other, the recruits spring up from within and among their families and close friends. In other words, once they are converted to Christianity, they are typically able to turn to those with whom they have already established strong bonds. As a result of the recruitment among those who share space and pre-existing intimate relationships, early Christianity emerged as an "intense community." It grew not because of the miracles that provided credibility, but rather because of invitations among friends, relatives, and neighbors.[37] The rise of Christianity numerically often does not occur as a result of mass conversions in response to a miracle, but rather, it grows out of interpersonal relationships.

Empowered by the Holy Spirit

The insights I have gained from the above scholars permit me to note that the main force of the Christian ministry is from the Holy Spirit. The book of Acts 2:41–47, further explains the process: "Those who accepted his message were baptized, and about three thousand were added to their number that day," and this led to "the breaking of bread and to prayer," and then "all the believers were together and had everything in common," and "every day they continued to meet together in the temple courts," then they "broke bread in their homes and ate together. And the Lord added to their numbers daily those who were being saved." The key words here are that,

36. Stark, *Rise of Christianity*, 20.
37. Stark, *Rise of Christianity*, 208.

"he added to their number daily" as they become the authentic Christian community. In other words, the Lord can "send" the authentic Christian community to the non-believers demonstrating the true Christianity which reflects God's attribution to the community.

The early church experienced phenomenal numerical growth through the acts of breaking bread together, sharing possessions, praising God, and enjoying the favor of all the people through the receiving of empowerment from the Holy Spirit. Individually, these activities were never to be the essence of ecclesiology. In one of his books, Stark describes the sociological reasons for growth in the early church, in addition to the organic relationship that causes numerical growth. Stark believes that another crucial reason for the increased numbers in the early church was because the communities shared perseverance and joy in their lives of faith.[38] Stark's discussion agrees with the discussion of Ephesians 4:11–13 (in Part I) in terms of highlighting the importance of inner growth in Christian lives.

Thus, if Christians are to be followers of Jesus, then we must live lives that are led by the Holy Spirit, and the fruit of the Spirit will inevitably overflow out of that into the world. Before we ask ourselves how we should be a Missional Church and how we can form a missional ecclesiology, it would be proper to first ask how we can be followers of Jesus in our everyday lives in order that we can be ready to be "sent out" to the community. Only then can we consider how to assess whether or not a community, congregation, and church are really growing, without focusing merely on a community's numerical growth. What is the relationship between forming community and discerning Christian growth? I see the answer in being pursuant of the fruit of the Holy Spirit and the eagerness and readiness of being a sent one.

Between Theory and Reality

If Christian theology and ecclesiology are formed around how the church developed historically rather than who God is, this can lead to a dangerous theology that is separate from the reality of everyday Christian life. During an interview with Alan Roxburgh in January of 2007, Ryan Bolger expressed concern about theological training that would be based on Christendom—which developed in the context of modernity.[39] This concern is helpful for us as I agree that there is often a struggle between learned theology—which

---

38. Stark, *Rise of Christianity*, 20–21.
39. See Roxburgh, "What is the Difference?"

is usually formed out of Christendom—and the reality of post-modern Christian discipleship.

The Marks of a Church

I believe ecclesiology is more than merely a particular theology or a summary of historical observations about how a church should be. Ecclesiology should also encompass and embrace prophetic observations on and visions of how the church should be in the future. When Jesus stated, "I will build my church," He was fully aware of what was and is to come. Jesus stands as our precedent in relation to both culture and the church. He not only knew how the church would be built and what elements would comprise the church, but He also knew how to prepare people to be the church in the cultural contexts that were to come. It is not fitting to build a church by way of looking inside an existing church and then imitating its patterns and structure in a new church. We need a way to anticipate what is coming in order to prepare the church to be a church in its full potential. Each century, Christians have carried specific missions of bringing the gospel to particular cultures, situations, and problems. The church can be built in the way that Jesus would build it if only the church is prepared for a *"kairos"* moment.[40] *"Kairos"* means, in Greek, a moment in time when something brand new can emerge. If the early church then was prepared, and the church now is not prepared for a *kairos* moment, then it cannot be the salt and light of the world it needs to be.

The current institutional or denominational leaders within North American Christianity were trained based on the above theology. Naturally, they responded by building a church based upon what they learned. Ironically, the sheep (the church-goers) began to try to correct the Shepherd's (the church leadership's) way of leading, because they believed that the Shepherds were going in the wrong direction—they tried to lead them in the Christian life by practicing theology.

The Marks of *Missio Dei*

Along with Anderson, David Bosch is alarmed at the lasting effects of doing theology and mission the wrong way. He interprets the *missio Dei* as

---

40. Anderson, *Emergent Theology for Emerging Churches*, 20–26.

Ecclesial Elements and Church Growth

representing God in the world, over representing God against the world. He goes on to make a contrast between simply doing "the planting of churches or the saving of souls," and being of "service to the *missio Dei*, representing God." He found that the *missiones ecclesia*, that is, the mission of the church, is only that of pointing to God.[41] For Bosch, mission needs to understand who God is, and the *missio Dei* as God the Father sending the Son. Therefore, the primary purpose of the church is to demonstrate God's love in and over the world.

Reflecting on both Anderson's and Bosch's insight on the purpose of the church, the life of a Christian is far more integral than any institutional or denominational function. As previously mentioned, if according to Gibbs, the context of Modernity and of Ecclesiology, or even Soteriology, can mislead a church to misunderstand the authentic meaning of the *missio Dei* as God the Father sending the Son, then searching for the mark of the *missio Dei* will be essential.[42] Where should we find the marks of *missio Dei*?

Wilbert Shenk brings a meaningful insight to the discussion of the disciple community,[43] which will relate to the issue of the marks of *missio Dei*. He presents Jesus the Messiah as the prototype for the mission. This is not just for the historical events, however, it is for the renewed meaning of the mission, "Disciple community."[44] He summarizes the "Disciple community" as follows:

> This calls for a theology of mission that makes the mission of Jesus Messiah the *sine qua non* of the nature and purpose of the church. The theology of *missio* should be integral to the entire theological enterprise. . . . An adequate theology of mission must be faithful to the fullness of the gospel. Only a theology based on the Kingdom of God present and coming, led by God's Messiah, is capable of holding the whole together.[45]

Thus, a mark of the *missio Dei* is to invite people to a new relationship creating a new community that is a reality. A discipling community is not a program but, rather, it is geared toward inviting others to a new order of reality.

41. Bosch, *Transforming Mission*, 390–91.
42. Gibbs, *Church NEXT*, 28–32.
43. Shenk, *Changing Frontiers of Mission*, 10–12.
44. Shenk, *Changing Frontiers of Mission*, 10.
45. Shenk, *Changing Frontiers of Mission*, 11.

In fact, as I observed previously, Van Engen also highlights the importance of missiology on a mission and the church. He continues:

> We hope that the new perspective of learn-from-each-other's church and mission definitely reject the *a priori* assumptions of the visible church like the IMC did back in 1957 in relation to the church and mission . . . the church's nature, reason for being, and mission in the world were progressively elaborated and shaped through missionary outreach. One of the reasons why modern ecclesiology was formed was that the many "interdenominational" or "non-denominational" churches have *forced* us to ask some very searching questions about the nature of the church.[46]

Similarly, I strongly believe that this new "wineskin," as Van Engen calls it, will find a way to hold new wine. How can it be true for us today when the sheep are already walking to a different path from their Shepherd? Who are the sheep today that would force the modern church to answer important questions about the nature of the church in the North American post-modern context?

In chapter 10, I will explore the two distinct phases of two particular church movements: the Missional Church and the Emerging Church. I will do this in order to envision how biblical Ecclesiology can cooperate with Christian "Reality" in the post-church growth era. In other words, I will try to identify the particular marks that each movement offers in order to realize a biblical church in the twenty-first-century North American context. By so doing, I hope to envision a way that the church can "become mature, attaining to the whole measure of the fullness of Christ" (Eph 4:13).

---

46. Van Engen, *God's Missionary People*, 38–40.

Chapter 10

Ecclesial Elements in the Broader Context: Emerging and Missional Church

"What makes the church the church?" and "Are we forming ecclesiologies in contemporary culture as Jesus would?" I will highlight these two questions in this chapter by examining the ecclesiological manifestations of two different missiological movements in North America, Emerging and Missional Churches. Along with my examination of the New Apostolic movement as represented by the case studies in Part II, these are two significant movements that have risen in the last thirty years contributing to church growth in the North American post-modern context.

I will explore the Emerging and Missional Church Movements respecting their strengths in order to envision a biblical Ecclesiology in the twenty-first century in North America. I will also draw attention to the fruits and marks of the Emerging and Missional Church Movements that are produced from the daily lives of the people within the movements. This exploration will suggest that each church movement reflects, in part, the biblical mode of being a church. As I present the Ecclesiology of these two missiological movements, I will gather parts and elements of their biblical nature. These parts and elements of their biblical nature can then be applied to strengthen the NARC as a demonstrated relevance of the charismatic environment just as the Missional and Emerging elements demonstrate denominational and evangelical contexts respectively.

Marks of the Emerging Church

The purpose of this brief exposition is to draw attention to the ecclesial elements of the Emerging Church paradigm in order to envision a biblical ecclesiology in the broader context. Thus, the strengths and fruits of the Emerging Church will be sought intentionally for the purpose of envisioning a biblical Ecclesiology in the twenty-first-century North American context.

Ecclesial Form of Emerging Church

John S. Hammett, a professor of Southeastern Baptist Theological Seminary, emphasizes the issue of "accuracy" as the central premise of the Emerging Church.[1] His main premise is that part of the church's calling is to respond to the culture, and in this case, to post-modernism. However, he over-emphasizes this point. I disagree with the concept that the central premise of the Emerging Church Movement is to respond to post-modernism *per se*. Rather, the Emerging Church is shaped by post-modernism, and acts as a "way of expressing that we need new forms of church that relate to the emerging culture."[2]

After five years of collecting data from current Emerging Churches, Gibbs and Bolger define the term *Emerging Church* as "communities that practice the way of Jesus within post-modern cultures."[3] As Gibbs and Bolger helpfully list, their definition incorporates nine practices:

> Emerging Churches: (1) identify with the life of Jesus, (2) transform the secular realm, and (3) live highly communal lives. Because of these three activities, they (4) welcome the stranger, (5) serve with generosity, (6) participate as producers, (7) create as created beings, (8) lead as a body, and (9) take part in spiritual activities.[4]

Of the nine practices, the emphasis is placed on the life of Jesus, transformation, and communal living. These, I believe, represent the Emerging Church's ecclesial form. Since they identify their own lives with the life of Jesus as they seek to transform the secular culture by living communally, this movement is better able to welcome the stranger, serve

---

1. Hammett, "Ecclesiological Assessment," 4.
2. Gibbs and Bolger, *Emerging Churches*, 41.
3. Gibbs and Bolger, *Emerging Churches*, 45.
4. Gibbs and Bolger, *Emerging Churches*, 45.

Ecclesial Elements in the Broader Context

with generosity, participate as producers, create as created beings, lead as a body, and take part in spiritual activities. Returning to Kärkkäinen's questions (that is, what makes the church the church, and what should form the ministry, structure, and sacraments of the church?), the above nine characteristics clearly help us as we consider these questions in order to understand Karkkainen's analysis of Ecclesiology.

Community as Fruits of the Emerging Church

The main posture of the Emerging Church is to identify with the life of Jesus. D. A. Carson explains some characteristics of that identity—that the Emerging Church is characterized by its protest against modernity, and by its conviction that churches must respond to changes in the post-modern culture.[5] However, this is secondary to the movement's primary posture.

In terms of the marginalized gospel in the Western context, Bolger states that "Modernity created a religious sphere and pushed the church to the periphery of society."[6] He goes on to situate this being on the periphery within the modern era in the West: "Church life remained at the margins of society, encapsulated with the religious sphere and addressing spiritual issues."[7] It was primarily explained as the replication of the Mission stations from McGavran's mission strategy. However, this replication, called fragmentation by Bolger (2007), led to the birth of the Emerging Church. If fragmentation separates Christianity from everyday life, then the Emerging Church returns its focus to everyday life within the cultures and beliefs that are to represent the "real church." Thus, one way the Emerging Church does this, is by resisting institutionalization and by coming out of the formal meetings that many modern churches have maintained.

D.A. Carson connects Hunter's "say-a-prayer-so-that–when-you-die-you-can-go-to-heaven"[8] phenomenon to Bolger's analysis. Cognizance should be taken of how reductionism focuses on the salvation prayer as a symbol of being Christian instead of focusing on the sanctifying life process that forms believers into being more like Jesus. Sadly, because of this, the importance of a Christians' everyday life has been largely ignored in modern Christianity.

---

5. Carson, *Becoming Conversant*, 41.
6. Bolger, "Practice Movements," 3.
7. Bolger, "Practice Movements," 3.
8. Carson, *Becoming Conversant*, 22.

Guder also agrees with Bolger's diagnosis of fragmentation in the modern period, which then causes the church to be marginalized from society. In Guder's theological view point, fragmentation can be defined as reductionism. He emphasizes:

> The risk of translatability is that sinful humans are its agents. The witnesses are always very ambiguous saints. They (we) never divorce themselves from the desire to bring this powerful and radical gospel under control. That means that in the process of translation, complex forms of reduction also take place.[9]

Through translation and reduction, the church unintentionally "reduces the gospel." Thus, when Christians try to communicate the gospel, in the process, they tend to put the gospel under the control of the cultural context[10] Bolger describes this biased lack of awareness among his theological students as a barrier to discerning what Jesus really meant in the text.

One significant outcome of reductionism is the lack of community. Following Bolger's analysis, the Emerging Church empowers the local church to help build community, as everyday life being lived out together in the community with great emphasis. This, then, represents the "real church."

Creating Contemporary Community as Strength

According to Carson, the Emerging Church is characterized by its protest against modernity and its corresponding conviction that churches must respond to the momentous changes in culture represented by post-modernism. Thus, I believe churches must respond to the fragmentation and reduction-oriented culture around them.[11]

What exactly is the Emerging Church doing that is different? How is it creating the kind of communities that we have been talking about? Reflecting on the work of the People Movement by Bolger may help us to see precisely how: first, by observing and then by engaging the already existing relational structures of a people group, in McGavran's case, India.[12]

---

9. Guder, *Continuing Conversion of the Church*, 97.
10. Guder, *Continuing Conversion of the Church*, 97–98.
11. Carson, *Becoming Conversant*, 41–42.
12. Bolger, "Practice Movements," 8.

Since Indian culture is highly group-oriented, the relational structures are already intact. McGavran's careful observations help Christians to adopt a strategy that is culturally appropriate to India. The structures of the church need to be organic within that particular culture. Both Gibbs and Bolger observe how the Emerging Churches skillfully achieved this throughout England and parts of North America.[13] Their guiding question was how this church would look if Jesus was establishing the church in this particular culture? This question allows for input from the cultures around a community of believers, thus creating churches that would likely merge well with the surrounding culture. While this is a very helpful insight for those focusing on group-oriented culture; in contrast, the relational structures are not already intact in North America, and the people are often isolated and without communities.

Thus, post-modern culture requires that the 'modernity-church' re-shape itself in order to be appropriate for post-modernized, organic, people movements in the church.[14] Since culture is "a way of life," the post-modern approach to Christianity has helped push the modernist mind-set of "mission station" out of North American churches. This means that Emerging Churches are creating the *kairos* moment in North America. This will produce the relational structures of a particular community in churches in North America so that a post-modern approach to ecclesiology surfaces. In other words, the Emerging Church is creating the necessary environment for the re-birth of new Christians in the post-modern culture who will engage their everyday lives in a particular community.

If identifying with the life of Jesus empowers local church communities to struggle, discern, and then to conform to what his community would look like, then all who profess to be his followers should emulate the example of the Emerging Church. In general, this is a forgotten lifestyle in present day ecclesial form. I believe it is in borrowing from the Emerging Church's example that Christians everywhere will begin to engage in a more communal lifestyle. Furthermore, I hope to better integrate the ecclesial form of the Emerging Church as I continue to envision what a "fuller" ecclesiology should look like based on the remaining fruits I see in the movement.

---

13. Gibbs and Bolger, *Emerging Churches*.
14. Bolger, "Practice Movements," 188.

Marks of the Missional Church

The purpose of this brief exploration is to identify with the biblical ecclesial elements of Missional Church in order to move toward biblical ecclesiology in twenty-first-century North America. Considering the fact that the background of the Missional Church is primarily based on existing denominational churches, the premier strength of ecclesial elements can be characterized as being sent.

Ecclesial Form of the Missional Church

If the Emerging Church is described as facing a moment [*kairos*], then the Missional Church can be described as "movement" according to Anderson's discussion on "moments" and "movements."[15] Anderson makes the insightful distinction between moments and movements which helps us to understand the different starting points of the Missional Church and the Emerging Church. He describes "movement" as the renewal force of existing churches—the "development of a new strain out of an older batch."[16] He provides an illustration from the early church to help demonstrate what he means: The church community in Jerusalem maintained a fair degree of continuity with the tradition of the Twelve disciples.[17] Following his logic then, the Emerging Church is more of a revolution than a movement, because it aims at producing "a new system and a new way of behaving rather than a new behavior within the same system."[18] On the contrary, the Missional Church brought the renewal of existing modern churches in North America with regard to doing missions as "being sent."

Van Engen states that the church changes naturally because "significant social and demographic factors affect growth."[19] To Van Engen, in this culture and time, the modern church is affected by post-modernism which then enables the modern church to process its own growth. In this case, the growth identifies that the church is being sent to another culture. Because of this renewal of the paradigm, theology in North America shifted from mission and theology to missional theology.[20]

15. Anderson, *Emergent Theology for Emerging Churches*, 20.
16. Anderson, *Emergent Theology for Emerging Churches*, 20–21.
17. Anderson, *Emergent Theology for Emerging Churches*, 20.
18. Anderson, *Emergent Theology for Emerging Churches*, 21.
19. Van Engen, *God's Missionary People*, 41.
20. Guder, "From Mission and Theology," 36–54.

Guder laid out a fair outline of how missional theology was born in North America by tracing the chronological order of various missional disciplines.[21] He states that "In spite of the fact that the subject of missions had been included in a variety of ways in the curricula of theological education since the early nineteenth century, the relationship between theology and missions was mainly seen as a matter of theory and practice."[22] This was one of the established points on the subject of missions in the 1960s. From there, theologians eventually arrived at the understanding that "missions are not secondary to its being; the church exists in being sent and is building itself up for the sake of its being."[23]

This definition is mainly based on the work of Karl Barth, even though he did not directly mention the Missional Church. Barth made a significant theological turn when he labeled soteriology as the justification, which enabled him to say, "The Holy Spirit and the gathering of the Christian community," "The Holy Spirit and the upbuilding of the Christian community."[24] This way of understanding is called missional theology and is foundational theology for the Missional Church.

Borrowing from Lois Y. Barrett's work, we are able to identify what makes the Missional Church, a church:

> Patterns of the Missional Church are (1) missional vocation, (2) biblical formation and discipleship, (3) taking risks as a contrast community, (4) practices that demonstrate God's intent for the world, (5) worship as public witness, (6) dependence on the Holy Spirit, (7) pointing toward the reign of God, and (8) missional authority.[25]

In other words, according to L. Barrett, the definition of a missional congregation is being shaped by participation in God's mission, so that God's mission can permeate everything that the congregation does—from worship to witnessing, to training members for discipleship. A missional congregation effectively bridges the gap between outreach and congregational life.[26]

---

21. Guder, "From Mission and Theology," 36–54.
22. Guder, "From Mission and Theology," 38.
23. Guder, "From Mission and Theology," 46.
24. Guder, "From Mission and Theology" 45–46.
25. Barrett, *Treasure in Clay Jars,* xii–xiv.
26. Barrett, *Treasure in Clay Jars,* x.

Renewal Paradigm of Missio Dei as Fruits

To participate in God's mission clearly suggests a strong renewal paradigm that the church is being sent to the world and that this outgoing is wrapped up in the nature and identity of the church. Bosch has noted that the church is seen, essentially, as a missionary movement.[27] This means that the church exists to send and to build up itself for the sake of its mission. It means also that it is not to be considered the work of the church, but rather, the duty of the church. This duty belongs to the whole church, not just to a part of it.

Van Engen agrees that the role of the local church in the world must be as missionary congregations in the Kingdom of God.[28] The church's identity as a missionary people is not merely an important side note for the church, but rather, in the truest sense of the word, it is the foundational essence for all missionary activities.

In short, the fruit of the Missional Church is that the church needs to be shaped by God's missional work in order to be "the church." According to Barrett, God's mission in the world is to restore things to the way God intended the world to be before it became broken and sinful.[29] God's mission is uniquely carried out by *being sent* into the world. This mission, highlighted in the Missional Church Movement, is the fruit of ecclesial form I would like to carry forward as I envision a biblical ecclesiology in the twenty-first century in North America.

Fruits from Emerging and Missional Churches

Recognizing the need to investigate new ecclesiological criteria was where I began in Part III: My interactions with modern Ecclesiology, McGavran's understanding of church growth, and then Bolger's interaction with McGavran's work, have only confirmed my initial belief in the need for further investigation. As I have researched, subsequent points that grew out of that premise have been shaped through my engagement with the work of others. The following points represent my attempt to consider all that should be entailed in "fruits from Emerging and Missional Churches" in order to envision a biblical ecclesiology in the twenty-first century in North America.

---

27. Bosch, *Transforming Mission*, 372.
28. Van Engen, *God's Missionary People*, 87–100.
29. Barrett, *Treasure in Clay Jars*, x.

Ecclesial Elements in the Broader Context

My own ecclesiology has been challenged through writing and researching as I have engaged in various ecclesial forms in order to appreciate what it would look like for the biblical church which is maturing to attain "the whole measure of the fullness of Christ" (Eph 4:13). In my observation of these contemporary movements, there were commonalities that led me to confirm my initial assumption. It is vital to create an environment for the re-birth of new Christians in a post-modern culture that will then engage the world in their everyday life within particular communities.

Even though the process of creating such communities often invites criticism from those outside the movements, it would be worth noting that Jesus experienced persecution and that Christians were told to expect it as well. What really matters here is whether or not these new movements will accomplish the mission. Regardless of criticism and suffering, Jesus concluded his life and ministry as a perfectionist; "It is finished" (John 19:30). Our task, as theologians, ecclesiologists, and missiologists is to usher Christians along to accomplish their work. Hearing from a group of leaders from the Emerging Church clarifies this need:

> Because most of us write as local church practitioners rather than professional scholars, and because professional scholars who criticize our work may find it hard to be convinced by people outside their guild, we feel it wisest at this juncture to ask those in the academy to respond to their peers about our work. We hope to generate fruitful conversations at several levels, including both the academic and ecclesial realms. If few in the academy come to our defense in the coming years, then we will have more reason to believe we are mistaken in our thinking and that our critics are correct in their unchallenged analyses.[30]

I value the intent of this statement, and I hope that we can begin the organic, bottom-up process of cultivating the theological community that they envision.

Figure 3 expresses how the church can move toward a biblical ecclesiology. Ecclesiology will not come into fullness until the individual recognizes the strengths and fruits of that broader context of their own movement. In conformity with Figure 3, the following six points are a summary of Part III, which serves as an expression of how the different movements of the body of Christ can weave a biblical ecclesiology by drawing inspiration from the best fruits of each movement while guarding against their mistakes.

30. Jones et al., "Our Response."

- The criteria of modern ecclesiology might not be appropriate for churches in North America operating in a post-modern context.
- Oftentimes, the culture serves as God's tool exposing non-biblical ecclesiology. In this way, culture might serve to assist biblical ecclesiology.
- Culture, as a way of life, can expose real spirituality and hints as to how Jesus would build his church.
- The new criteria for church growth will be shaped by this new ecclesiology.
- Similar to the process of blending missions and theology to become missional theology, it might be possible to move from missional theology and ecclesiology to a missional ecclesiology that highlights *missio Dei* in the contemporary North American context.
- Everyday life will be the most important quality when the focus is on being sent to a particular community within the post-modern context.
- When we live lives similar to Jesus in a particular community, our individual faith and character can become a tool for the community.

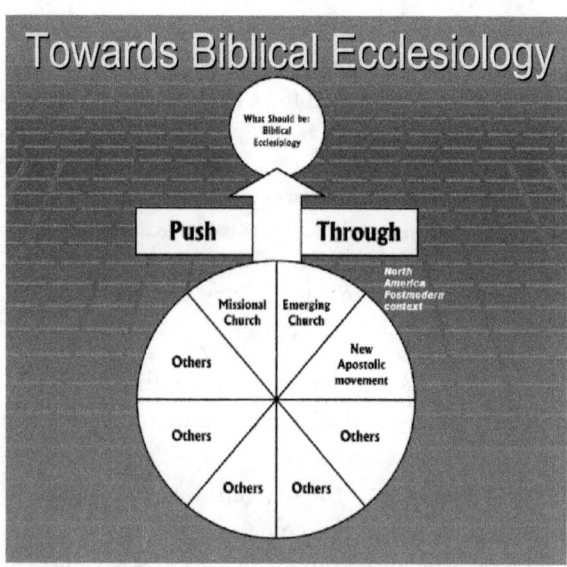

Figure 3
Moving Toward Biblical Ecclesiology

Moving Toward a Twenty-First-Century Apostolic Leadership and Ministry

As noted previously, each movement has its own assumptions relating to ecclesiology that were formed out of an ecclesial response to contemporary culture. The Emerging Church has a communal ecclesiology. The Missional Church holds to an Institutional ecclesiology. And the New Apostolic Reformation Church has assumptions that relate to the moving of the Holy Spirit. As I move toward a twenty-first-century Apostolic Church, along with the Emerging and Missional Church, I will try to position the Apostolic Church as a part of global Christianity by first bringing others into the picture, and then, position the Apostolic Church accordingly.

Table 12
Comparison of the Three Movements

	Emerging Church (EC)	Missional Church (MC)	New Apostolic Reformation Church (NARC)
Strength; Fruits	• Identify with the life of Jesus • Live highly communal lives • Welcome the stranger in their community • Serve with generosity • Take part in spiritual activities	• Renewal paradigm of *missio Dei* • Transforming churches towards the mission • MC seeks to discern God's specific missional vocation for the entire community and for all of its members • Missional community is indicated by how Christians behave toward one another	• Gift based (Eph 4:11), • Equipping the saints • The priesthood of all believers. • Focus on pioneering church • Recognize apostleship as leadership • Try to practice the concept of 'send one' • Focus on the Holy Spirit
Mistakes (which need to avoided)	• Lack of leadership structure • Weak point on the pioneering church	• Rigid, modern culture. • Authoritarian • institutional	• Its vision has been skewed by Apostle-centric ecclesiology. • There is a huge gap between theory and reality
Why	Post-modern resistance to authority and rigid structure. Strong cultural influence.	The structure and life of church derived from the hierarchical cultural milieu of modernity.	Peter Wagner used the term apostolos or Apostles to describe church leadership and structure, rather than to describe church mission and the "sent ones" or missionaries to the unbelieving world.

As shown in Table 11, the strength of the EC is to create the community in a 24/7 church culture. EC focuses largely on character, compassion, and caring for people within the ecclesial community. However, the weakness of EC remains in the areas of lack of leadership structure, and no emphasis on the pioneering church. The main reason why the strengths and also weaknesses are manifested in that particular way is a reaction to mega-church structure, authority, and programs while being sensitive to postmodern culture.

The strength of the MC is that it focuses on the renewal paradigm of *missio Dei*. MC seeks to transform churches toward the mission and also to discern God's specific missional vocation for the entire community and for all of its members.[31] MC's weaknesses emphasize a focus on authoritarian leadership and institutional structure. The structure and life of the church are derived from the hierarchical cultural milieu of modernity.

The strength of the New Apostolic Reformation Church (NARC) is its focused vision: pursuing the five-fold, gift-based ministry (Eph 4:11) by equipping the saints, and the priesthood of all believers. However, weaknesses result from the very vision on which this movement is based, namely Apostle-centered ecclesiology. There is a remarkable gap between theory and reality in terms of casting their theory and vision into practice. C. Peter Wagner used the term *apostolos* or Apostles to describe church leadership and structure, rather than to describe church mission and the "sent ones" or missionaries to the unbelieving world. In theory, a Holy-Spirit centered vision should have generated a leadership or church structure that placed emphasis on the gifts as they impact the ministry of the church to the world. In reality, however, the NARC basically inherited from the Missional Church an institutional and hierarchical legacy. When this became baptized with the "power of the Holy Spirit" as manifested through the central figures of this new Holy Spirit movement, an Apostle-centered leadership was born. By so doing, the authority was further concentrated and consolidated on an "Apostle."

Considering the fact that the center of biblical ecclesiology is the Kingdom of God or the Reign of God (Matt 3:2), a biblical ecclesiology assumes that this invitation is still valid and the Kingdom of God is still at hand. It also assumes that one enters this Kingdom through Jesus Christ and Him alone, not by fellowship, not by institutional life, and not even by the power ministry. Christ's church was founded by and continues to exist in and

---

31. Gibbs, *Church NEXT*, 201.

through Him, who indwells his body in the person of the Holy Spirit. That biblical ecclesiology is Kingdom-centered means that the Church exists to advance the Kingdom or reign of God by being sent like Jesus (John 20:21). This understanding of being sent ones is a key to enhance the effectiveness of missions in the twenty-first-century church. The biblical church that is apostolic needs to be reaffirmed and recognized by bringing a biblical meaning of apostle as a "sent one." Thus, the Apostolic Church should position itself to bring both mission and church together into the churches in the twenty-first century as a part of global missional Christianity.

Summary

In Part III, I have presented a broader church context that provides one of the tools to understanding a biblical ecclesiology. The Emerging Church can be seen as "ambivalent" in terms of being contrary to institutionalized mega-churches in North America. Their main ecclesial fruits reflect a biblical way of community life, worship, and sharing, through their unique post-modern expression of art, music, and lifestyle in small community settings.

On the other hand, the fruit of Missional Churches communicates *missio Dei* as a renewed sense of missions in the church. The main strength of Missional Churches is to reproduce mission faithfully in existing denominations across North America. The commonality of both Emerging and Missional Churches is a recognition of the need to move beyond Christendom and modern ecclesiology.

Moving beyond Christendom and modern ecclesiology means: first, that post-modern Christians will need to pay closer attention to a more basic, Christo-centric, and post-Christendom ecclesiology; and second, that Christians must continue to envision ways to weave together an authentic and culturally relevant ecclesiology in the North American post-modern context, drawing inspiration from the best fruits of each other's movements, yet avoiding each other's mistakes. In other words, the un-biblical-centered tendency of the NARC will be redefined when she gives special attention to other movements' biblical expression of the twenty-first-century contemporary church. Both the Emerging and Missional Churches pursue the reinstatement of biblical ecclesiology. The Emerging Church calls for the biblical meaning of being Christians through authentic fellowship. Their understanding of being a church enhances the characteristics of the early church as sharing love with each other in everyday life. Missional Church also expresses a renewed understanding of God's attributes. The Missional Church calls the church to recognize the biblical purpose of being a church. To sum up, the biblical meaning of an Apostolic Church has much of its value in the synthesis of both the mission and the church. If the modern church separates mission and the church, then, the post-modern church puts an intentional focus on bringing missions back into the church. The Emerging Church movement contributes to the "lifestyle" model of missional and biblical ecclesiology. The Missional Church movement shows its strength in re-focusing the purpose of the church through re-defining *missio Dei*. Consequently, biblical apostolic leadership plays a crucial role in missional ecclesiology.

Recommendations

BASED ON BIBLICAL CONTEXTS, my research within the NARC and in two missiological movements as a broader context in North America, I suggest the following recommendations in conclusion. These recommendations are based solely on my findings on the three NARC case studies. Therefore, it is important to verify my findings with a much broader sample.

In this section, the significant statement of chapter 1 will be restated as I will make relevant and viable recommendations in terms of bringing about a vibrant twenty-first-century Apostolic Church that is biblically missional, theologically profound, and culturally relevant. First, I will encourage the relevant and vibrant twenty-first-century Apostolic Church to blend with the early church life which was defined in chapter 1 in both Tables 1 (Critique Framework for Apostle) and 2 (Critique Framework for Biblical Ecclesiology). Secondly, as a product of applying the first point, this research will be able to position the Apostolic Church as a part of global Christianity, along with the Emerging and Missional Churches, as a whole. The relevant and vibrant Apostolic Church will be positioned and recognized as one of the Christian cultures in the body of Christ in twenty-first-century North American Christianity. This will be in terms of enhanced effectiveness of missions and reaffirming the biblical purpose of being the church, as highlighted in Part III.

Biblical Ecclesiology and Biblical Apostolic Church

I will make recommendations in five areas to express the relevant and vibrant Apostolic Church and also to bring the early church life as shown in Table 1 and Table 2; leadership, life of the church, mission, Holy Spirit, and church growth.

A 21st-Century Biblical, Apostolic Church

Leadership

Based on Ephesians 4:11–13, according to Table 1 (see p. 15), the church embraces a five-fold ministry which recognizes a biblical meaning of apostle as "sent one." Ephesians 4:11–13 defines the apostolic gift as foundational leadership, but not in a dictatorial form. Irrespective of how powerfully one demonstrates his or her spiritual gifts and ministers effectively, no one person in the body of Christ can assume the kind of authority and accountability that Christ exercised. Even his twelve apostles were sent out in pairs—a proof of the incompleteness of one person, regardless of the level of power, gifts, and authority. Both Christ and Paul recognized that the ultimate leader of the body of Christ is Christ himself and the church leadership is comprised of people with different gifts, who together make up a more complete leadership core (1 Pet 2:9; 1 Cor 12:27–31).

While we may see the relationship of Christ to church leaders as a top-down model, the image of the body having many parts, gifts, and functions that are mutually dependent upon one another does not allow for a top-down understanding of leadership within the church or within the leadership (1 Cor 12:12–31).

This means, while Ephesians 4:11–13 still recognizes a place for a top or apostolic leader, this top leader must function with accountability and mutual submission to other leaders or offices (prophet, pastor, teacher, and evangelist). Thus, an apostolic leadership is functional (job descriptive), and it does not reflect any kind of ontological, positional, or functional superiority. Ontologically speaking, one could argue that the five-fold ministries are all equal in importance. If one is exalted above the other, it is an invitation to the corruption of gift and power. Thus, the apostolic leaders need to function in accountability to, partnership with, and mutual submission to other offices or gifts. Each gift or office functions uniquely and equally contribute to the whole of the leadership, and each shape and sharpen the other.

Life of the Church

The five-fold ministry gifts in Ephesians 4:11–13, are fully functioning in building up the body, with a strong emphasis in teaching and discipleship in a corporate way. Thus, they expect individuals to bear the fruits of the Holy Spirit and demonstrate a vision for mission both in the community and in the world. Interdependence and accountability are needed in leadership for mutual coherence and member relationships. Furthermore, the life of the church will become a vibrant tool to presenting God's attributes to the non-believing extended family. This means that the life of the church is being sent out to the community and the world to participate in God's mission.

Mission

In its mission to both the immediate community and the world-wide community, the church must recognize and maintain the distinction between the church and the world, while being in the world. If it fails so to do, it loses the very thing that makes the church what it should be. This distinction is critical, not for the purpose of separating and privatizing faith, but precisely for the purpose of being effective as the light in darkness and salt in a decaying world. The church is therefore in the community, not only for fellowship and acts of compassion and service but also for presenting the Word and demonstrating the power of the Holy Spirit. In other words, the relevant and vibrant biblical mission is not limited to planting churches or saving souls, but also to being ambassadors who represent God. Thus, a relevant and vibrant Apostolic Church is not merely establishing churches that are planted in the community as symbols of the mission, but introducing God himself to the community as being the sender. This "being sent" aspect will be done by bringing apostolic gifts back to the church. The apostolic gifts will be placed in the church along with prophets, evangelists, teachers, and pastors.

Holy Spirit

As one would expect in a charismatic ecclesial context, one of the characteristics of the NARC is her emphasis on the Holy Spirit. This is in stark contrast with the previous church growth theory which emphasizes numeric growth and the number of commitments made to Christ. In theory, within the NARC movement, the emphasis is on the Holy Spirit, and growth has nothing to do with the number of new decisions made for Christ or for church attendance. But in reality, sometimes there has been a focus on mass evangelization and new decisions related to numerical church growth. Yet there is a need for pneumatology and the theory of church growth within the NARC that must be merged and emphasized from a biblical standpoint. This way, emphasis will not be on numbers, but on the growth and fruits of inner spiritual being (Eph 4:13).

Church Growth

The criteria of modern church ecclesiology might not be appropriate for the church in North America operating in a post-modern context. In order for the church to grow, ecclesiology and missional theology must be brought together to create a missional ecclesiology that highlights *missio Dei* in a contemporary context. The present church is a very established institution. However, the life of Jesus is not demonstrated in communal lives. The life of the Apostolic Church needs to combine the key elements of both the missional and emerging manifestations of contemporary churches in order to represent true light and salt by making church life not only an institutional organization but also a highly communal and deeply involved group of believers in the community.

The church must become an integral part of the community by welcoming strangers and "outcasts," by serving the needy in the community with generosity, by becoming productive members of the community, by setting godly trends in the community, by fully exploring God-given creativity in music, arts, business, and any other relevant expression for the community in which it serves. This way, the church will be serving like Christ, leading and setting the spiritual atmosphere for the community.

In short, this is a biblical model that is transferable from culture to culture. I am suggesting that this model is especially relevant to contemporary context because of resistance to form, authority, and institutions. With the biblical apostolic model as a foundation, with its strengths and weaknesses and in the light of other models, the new biblical missional ecclesiology that I envision would be a radically improved version of the NARC model, which I call a biblical ecclesiology, based on Ephesians 4:11–13; to become mature, attaining to the whole measure of the fullness of Christ.

Conclusion

The research represented in this book was dedicated to an exploration of the NARC's theoretical and phenomenological resources as a tool to enhance a biblical ecclesiology that is apostolic within the twenty-first-century North American church. I have achieved the process of exploring first, through

Recommendations

critiquing the NARC's theory and reality in light of biblical perspectives. I acknowledge, however, that the findings are based solely on three NARCs. By exploring this contrast, I identified a gap between theory and reality within the NARC through actual case studies of three NARCs. Finally, I have explored the Emerging and Missional models to see how various communities are forming biblical ecclesiology in twenty-first-century North America as well as blending their strengths to develop a biblical Apostolic Church that will enable the evangelization of the peoples of the world.

In the transition from the modern to post-modern, three new movements have been born in North America: the Missional, Emerging, and New Apostolic movements. Common to all these movements is the desire to go beyond ecclesial expressions of modernity. Each movement pushed themselves out of the modern model of doing church and moved toward a biblical model of expressing the body of Christ in contemporary society. A distinctive characteristic of these three movements is their high value on their own interpretation of what it means to be the church in a particular context. In other words, each movement struggled through their own way to be the church as it relates to a particular expression of faith: denominational, evangelical, and charismatic. As a result of their struggles, they demonstrate their relevance through unique ecclesial elements and distinctive spiritual phenomena. In reference to the previous highlights at the end of chapter 10, the "lifestyle" model of Emerging Churches and "re-focusing" *missio Dei* model of Missional Churches has much value to NARC in putting forth a biblical model of being a church in a contemporary context.

My primary critique of the current NARC is that as a movement it has not defined Apostle in a manner in keeping with the intent of scripture, namely with a focus on sending. Instead, the NARC has emphasized apostolic leadership resulting in a hierarchical structure that serves to focus on institutional development, the exact opposite of what the other movements (Missional and Emerging Churches), are endeavoring to achieve. Although NARC recognizes the crucial role of apostle in the church, NARC fails to practice the concept of "sending." While the first and foremost element of a biblical definition of apostle is found in the meaning of "sending," the gap between theory and reality within NARC serves to emphasize the non-biblical implementation of "being an apostle." Clearly, the biblical apostle is one who is sent by God, not the one who will send out other people. At the same time, the purpose of a biblical Apostolic Church is being sent to the world rather than simply being a sending agency. Thus, when the current NARC begins to emphasize the biblical function of apostle within the network of NARCs, the attributes of missional focus will be greater globally and thereby contribute to the expansion of Christ's body.

On the whole, in order to move toward a twenty-first-century biblical ecclesiology, churches need to stand on the biblical podium cultivating their reflection on building up the body of Christ together, not alone (Phil 2:3). If churches lose track of biblical exposure, it will look like that homeless woman who is a human being, yet did not look like a human being. Just as that homeless woman could not function as a human being, she was not to be treated as a human being, either. Similarly, each church movement needs to stand on the biblical stage in order to cultivate its own way of being the church. Thus, by acknowledging each other's strengths and weaknesses of being a church in the twenty-first-century North America, biblical ecclesiology will be enhanced. While biblical leadership is apostolic in the sense of sending, apostolic leadership is crucial if the church brings mission and ecclesiology together through the power of the Holy Spirit. A biblical ecclesiology is apostolic and must restate the sending mission in ecclesial elements.

Appendix A

An Inquiry About "Apostolic Church Case Study"

Dear Dr. Peter Wagner,

Greetings from a Fuller Theological Seminary student! I am SuYeon Yoon, a Ph.D. student at Fuller Seminary under Dr. Daniel Shaw, Dr. Eddie Gibbs, and Dr. Ryan Bolger. I am writing this email to inquire your suggestion for my research, "Missional Ecclesiology Among New Apostolic Reformation Churches in the North America Post-Modern Context":

I strongly agree that "we need to work out links in our **apostolic theology**; we need to compile **case studies of fruitful apostolic ministry**."[1] I am about to do a case study for the apostolic ministry. **Would you be able to suggest several fruitful apostolic ministries in the United States for my case studies?**

Thank you very much for your time and blessings on your ministry! Please do not hesitate to contact me either via email or phone if you have further questions.

Sincerely,
SuYeon Yoon,
Campus Minister, Harvest Rock Church, Pasadena, CA.

1. Wagner, *Changing Church*, 13

Appendix B

Case Study Cite:
A Letter From C. Peter Wagner

Dear SuYeon:

I am delighted that you are doing a study on Apostolic Churches with Eddie Gibbs. As case studies, I would suggest that you research:

- Michael Fletcher of Grace Churches International, Fayetteville, North Carolina;
- your own friend Ché Ahn, Pasadena, CA;
- Barbara Yoder of Ann Arbor, Michigan;
- Jim Hodges of Duncanville, Texas;
- Bill Hamon of Santa Rosa Beach, Florida; and
- Mel Mullen of Red Deer, Alberta, Canada (since your title is "North American," not just the USA.)

All of these apostles know each other and Ché is a friend of all of them as well.

If you need contact information, my assistant, Janine Cave, will be happy to provide the information for you.

Blessings,

C. Peter Wagner

Appendix C

Record of Data for Semi-Structured Interviews

Case/ Identification number		Age range	Gender	Years at case	Interview Date	Case study name	Tape #[1]	Primary context/Other pertinent information
1.	CS1-Int1	50–55	F	8	04.25.2007	MP1[2]	T-2	Pastoral staff member of Manna Church
2.	CS1-Int2	50–55	M	8	04.25.2007	MP2	T-1	Pastoral staff member of Manna Church
3.	CS1-Int3	35–40	M	10	04.25.2007	MP3	T-2	Pastoral staff member of Manna Church
4.	CS1-Int4	30–35	M	10	04.25.2007	MP4	T-2	Pastoral staff member of Manna Church
5.	CS1-Int5	45–50	M	9	04.25.2007	MP5	T-2	Pastoral staff member of Manna Church
6.	CS1-Int6	30–35	M	9	04.26.2007	MP6	T-2	Pastoral staff member of Manna Church
7.	CS1-Int7	25–30	F	2	04.26.2007	MC1[3]	T-3	Cell leader of Manna Church
8.	CS1-Int8	25–30	M	1	04.26.2007	MC2	T-3	Cell leader of Manna Church
9.	CS1-Int9	25–30	M	1	04.26.2007	MC3	T-3	Cell leader of Manna Church

2. Interview location in the cassette tape/total 11 tapes
3. MP=Manna Church Pastor
4. MC=Manna Church Cell leader

Case/ Identification number	Age range	Gender	Years at case	Interview Date	Case study name	Tape #[1]	Primary context/Other pertinent information
10. CS1-Int10	35–40	F	2	04.26.2007	MP7	T-2	Pastoral staff member of Manna Church
11. CS2-Int11	40–45	F	8	05.28.2007	WP[4]1	T-4	Pastoral staff member of Word of Life Church
12. CS2-Int12	30–35	M	8	05.28.2007	WP2	T-4	Pastoral staff member of Word of Life Church
13. CS2-Int13	50–55	M	10	05.29.2007	WP3	T-4/T-5	Pastoral staff member of Word of Life Church
14. CS2-Int14	50–55	F	10	05.29.2007	WP4	T-4/T-5	Pastoral staff member of Word of Life Church
15. CS2-Int15	30–35	M	9	05.29.2007	WP5	T-5	Pastoral staff member of Word of Life Church
16. CS2-Int16	30–35	M	9	05.29.2007	WP6	T-6	Pastoral staff member of Word of Life Church
17. CS2-Int17	30–35	F	2	05.29.2007	WP7	T-6	Pastoral staff member of Word of Life Church
18. CS2-Int18	30–35	M	8	05.29.2007	WP8	T-6	Pastoral staff member of Word of Life Church
19. CS2-Int19	30–35	M	8	05.29.2007	WP9	T-6	Pastoral staff member of Word of Life Church
20. CS2-Int20	35–40	M	10	05.29.2007	WP10	T-6	Pastoral staff member of Word of Life Church
21. CS2-Int21	30–35	F	10	05.30.2007	WP11	T-6	Pastoral staff member of Word of Life Church
22. CS3-Int22	40–45	M	4	10.16.2007	BP[5]1	T-7	Pastoral staff member of Bethel World Outreach Center Church
23. CS3-Int23	55–60	M	1	10.16.2007	BP2	T-7	Pastoral staff member of Bethel World Outreach Center Church
24. CS3-Int24	40–45	M	ND	10.16.2007	BP2	T-7	Pastoral staff member of Bethel World Outreach Center Church
25. CS3-Int25	50–55	M	3	10.17.2007	BP3	T-7	Pastoral staff member of Bethel World Outreach Center Church

4. WP=Word of Life Church Pastor
5. BP=Bethel World Outreach Church Pastor

Record of Data for Semi-Structured Interviews

Case/ Identification number	Age range	Gender	Years at case	Interview Date	Case study name	Tape #[1]	Primary context/Other pertinent information
26. CS3-Int26	35–40	M	3	10.17.2007	BP3	T-7	Pastoral staff member of Bethel World Outreach Center Church
27. CS3-Int27	35–40	M	1	10.22.2007	BP4	T-8	Pastoral staff member of Bethel World Outreach Center Church
28. CS3-Int28	50–55	M	4	10.23.2007	BP5	T-8	Pastoral staff member of Bethel World Outreach Center Church
29. CS3-Int29	45–50	M	2	10.23.2007	BP6	T-8	Pastoral staff member of Bethel World Outreach Center Church
30. CS3-Int30	30–35	M	1	10.23.2007	BP7	T-8	Pastoral staff member of Bethel World Outreach Center Church
31. CS3-Int31	30–35	M	6	10.23.2007	BP8	T-8	Pastoral staff member of Bethel World Outreach Center Church
32. CS3-Int32	30–35	M	6	10.24.2007	BP9	T-9	Pastoral staff member of Bethel World Outreach Center Church
33. CS3-Int33	25–30	M	5	10.24.2007	BP10	T-9	Pastoral staff member of Bethel World Outreach Center Church
34. CS3-Int34	40–45	M	8	10.24.2007	BP11	T-9	Pastoral staff member of Bethel World Outreach Center Church
35. CS3-Int35	40–45	M	9	10.24.2007	BP12	T-9	Pastoral staff member of Bethel World Outreach Center Church
36. CS3-Int36	45–50	M	5	10.24.2007	BP13	T-9	Pastoral staff member of Bethel World Outreach Center Church
37. CS3-Int37	50–55	M	8	10.24.2007	BP14	T-9	Pastoral staff member of Bethel World Outreach Center Church

Case/ Identification number		Age range	Gender	Years at case	Interview Date	Case study name	Tape #[1]	Primary context/Other pertinent information
38.	CS3-Int38	50–55	M	10	10.25.2007	BP15	T-11	Pastoral staff member of Bethel World Outreach Center Church
39	CS3-Int39	45–50	M	10	10.25.2007	BP16	T-9 T-10	Pastoral staff member of Bethel World Outreach Center Church

Appendix D

Interview Questionnaire for Manna Church

1. How would you describe the Apostolic Ministry?

2. How did you plant Manna Church? [history/context/vision]

3. What is a key factor for decision making?
    - Selecting a team member
    - Ministry goals
    - Everyday life decisions

4. Would you articulate what made a shift from "home group" to "cell group"?

Appendix E

Interview Questionnaire for Michael Fletcher of Manna Church

1. How would you describe the Apostolic Ministry?

2. How did you plant Manna Church? [history/context/vision]

3. What is a key factor for the decision making?
    - Selecting a team member
    - Ministry goals
    - Everyday life decisions

4. Would you articulate what made a shift from "home group" to "cell group"?

5. Do you have an accountability group?

Appendix F

Interview with Mel Mullen

1. How would you describe the Apostolic Ministry?

Transcribe: The definition of being Apostolic
The definition of Apostle: vision and strategy oriented pastor

2. How did you plant Word of Life Church? [history/context/vision]

Transcribe: Kingdom of God
Destiny both individual and cooperate
Environment of grace: not religious—Not controlling, release them based on Eph 2:11, holding them loosely, let them make mistakes
Rich Culture

3. What is a key factor for decision making?
- Selecting a team member
- Ministry goal
- Everyday life decision

4. Do you have an accountability group?

Appendix G

Interview with Word of Life Church

1. How would you define/describe the Apostolic Ministry?

[Just for your reference, here's "Nine characteristics of the Apostolic Ministry" defined by C. Peter Wager.]

- New name.
- New authority structure / Led by "charismatic" pastor-leaders / Vision for what people can come.
- New leadership training / Strong lay ministries / Every member and every seeker receives regular pastoral care from a layperson.
- New ministry focus / Small groups / Family feeling, but not exclusive
- New worship style.
- New prayer forms/ Earnest in prayer
- New financing.
- New outreach / Many ministries to the unchurched / Cultural adaptation to the target population
- New power priorities / Passion for the outpouring of God's Spirit.

2. How did you find your spiritual gifts?

3. What is the most important reason to choose your team member OR ministry team?

4. What is the process of making a decision in your ministry?

Appendix H

Interview with Rice Broocks

- About empowerment: the Role of Apostle - Distinguishing between Apostolic and missional
- Seminary training vs. EN training
- What kind of theological training did you receive? Describe the impact of your theological training with practice in the field.
- What calling did you receive? What was the motivation for going to Seminary?
- After Seminary, what were the differences in terms of doing ministry?
- When is the first time using the term "apostle" versus "apostolic" Why?
- What is the impact of being "apostolic?"
- What are the main factors for church growth?
- Why did you decide to have multi-locations for your church?

Appendix I

Interview Questionnaire for Bethel World Outreach Center

1. Currently [at Bethel]
   - How many years?
2. Previously [before Bethel]
   - Education background
3. Interview Focus
   - What is church?
   - Define, "being apostolic"
   - The difference between apostolic and missional
   - The thoughts related to the breakdown of "The World Of 10"
   - Best thing about Bethel, and . . .
   - Introduce the six locations of WOC
   - What is your strength? How do others think of your strength?
   - The meaning of "Walking with Jesus."

Note regarding "The World of Ten"
Posted by Rice on Jul 25, 2007, 1:41 AM. for everyone "a minute with rice" There were many remarks made about an example I used in my conference message on Sat. night, "to the ends of the earth." These comments centered around the example of how the world really looks when reduced to ten

Interview Questionnaire for Bethel World Outreach Center

people. This example was referred to by Bill and Amy Stearns in their book, "20/20 vision." The example was originally used by a speaker they heard at a missions conference in Colorado Springs.

Before I explain it here in this post, let me echo the amazing reports of all that God is doing around the world. Though the lack of growth in the western world has led many to assume that Christianity is declining, the worldwide picture offers great hope. A quick report: 74,000 people are coming to Christ every day. Over 3,500 churches are opening worldwide every week. There are hundreds of testimonies of people in the Muslim world being converted because of a vision or dream of Jesus Christ. Africa is almost 50 percent Christian! However, there is much work to be done.

If you broke the world down into ten people, here is what you would have:

There is one committed believer. This is a genuine follower and disciple of Jesus Christ. There are two nominal believers. These are people who would profess some type of affinity to the Christian religion, but not be genuinely converted.(For those that might be confused, being a true follower of Christ doesn't depend on joining a particular church or denomination, but is a result of trusting Christ alone as your Savior and Lord and his death on a cross and subsequent resurrection from the dead three days later. He promised that we would be "born again" (John 3:1–7; 2 Corinthians 5:17).

There are four out of ten that are unreached (non-Christian) from nations that are potentially open in the sense that there is a Christian witness or ministry that could make contact with them. These four might be pictured as an Indian (India will pass China as the world's largest nation in 2015). A Chinese. China is approaching 10 percent Christian, but with over a billion people there is a vast sea of humanity that must be reached. A Japanese. Japan has over 130 million people and very little Gospel witness. A Thai. The word "Thai" ironically means "free." Thailand is opening up to the Gospel, but there are very few laborers for the harvest.

The last three of the ten are from nations that are "officially" closed to the Gospel. This would be the nations in the Muslim world. Though the church once flourished in this part of the world two millennia ago, the Light has grown dim. Many refuse to call them "closed" nations, but rather use the term, CAN (Creative Access Nations). Indeed, it will take enormous creativity and courage to see inroads made in these places.

The point is that there is a huge responsibility on the "one" to make a difference in the other "nine." The two nominal believers must be awakened in this crucial time, and help reach the four from the nations that are within reach right now. *Every Nation* has established ministries in all of these four regions. Our pastor in Japan, Scott Douma is on Multiply. Pastor Kevin Menezes in India, and the ministries in China and Thailand can be contacted through the Every Nation website. We will continue to press the issue until we reach "every nation in our generation!"

Appendix J

Interview Assessment

- Leader/Apostle's role: How are they impact way things done?
- What indicators emerge?
- Where indicators show up?
- Who is the around apostle enable apostle to do his job?
- Interview apostle: what they saying are true in their ministry?
- Motivation of ministry [history/context/vision]
  - How do they/apostles plant the church?
  - What was a key factor for the decision making?
  - How dreams/visions/signs/wonders/miracle/Holy Spirit guidance/prophetic words [supernatural intervention] plays in their decision making?
- Why do they decide to build NARC as it is in terms of setting a mission statement?
  - destiny
  - calling
  - mandate
- How do they set a boundary for the upcoming/direction of ministry?
- Testing value of mission statement: by forming middle level leaders group as a focus group

- How do they pick their team-things that they look for as qualifications of being a leader?
    - degree
    - gift
    - anointing

Bibliography

Agnew, Francis H. "The Origin of the NT Apostle-Concept: A Review of Research." *Journal of Biblical Literature* 105 (1986) 75–96.
Allen, Roland. *The Ministry of the Spirit*. London: World Dominion, 1960.
———. *Missionary Method: St. Paul's or Ours?* Grand Rapids, MI: Eerdmans, 1962.
Anderson, Ray S. *An Emergent Theology for Emerging Churches*. Downers Grove, IL: InterVarsity, 2006.
Banks, Robert. *Paul's Idea of Community: The Early House Churches in Their Historical Setting*. Grand Rapids, MI: Eerdmans, 1980.
Barrett, C. K. *A Commentary on the First Epistle to the Corinthians*. New York: Harper & Row, 1968.
Barrett, Lois Y., ed. *Treasure In Clay Jars: Patterns in Missional Faithfulness*. Grand Rapids, MI: Eerdmans, 2004.
Betz, Hans Dieter. "Apostle" In *The Anchor Bible Dictionary*, edited by David Noel Freedman, 309–11. Vol. 1. New York: Doubleday, 1992.
Bolger, Ryan K. "Practice Movements in Global Information Culture: Looking Back to McGavran and Finding a Way Forward." *Missiology* 35.2 (2007) 181–93.
Bosch, David J. *Transforming Mission: Paradigm Shifts in Theology of Mission*. Maryknoll, NY: Orbis, 2002.
Breen, Mike. *The Apostle's Notebook*. Eastbourne, England: Kingsway, 2002.
Bruce, F. F. *The Epistle to the Colossians, to Philemon, and to the Ephesians*. Grand Rapids, MI: Eerdmans, 1984.
Cannistraci, David. *Apostles and the Emerging Apostolic Movement*. Ventura, CA: Renew, 1998.
———. *The Gift of Apostle: A Biblical look at Apostleship and How God is using it to bless His Church Today*. Ventura, CA: Regal, 1996.
Carson, D. A. *Becoming Conversant with the Emerging Church: Understanding a Movement and Its Implications*. Grand Rapids, MI: Zondervan, 2005.
Carson, D. A., Douglas J. Moo, and Leon Morris. *An Introduction to the New Testament*. Grand Rapids, MI: Zondervan, 1991.
Collins, Raymond F. *First Corinthians*. Collegeville, MN: Liturgical, 1999.
Dunn, James D. G. *Jesus Remembered*. Vol. 1 of *Christianity in the Making*. Grand Rapids, MI: Eerdmans, 2003.
Dunn, James D. G., and Doris Donnelly, eds. *Jesus: A Colloquium in the Holy Land*. New York: Continuum, 2001.
———. *Jesus and the Spirit: A Study of the Religious and Charismatic Experience of Jesus and the First Christians as Reflected in the New Testament*. Philadelphia: Westminster, 1975.

Bibliography

Eckhardt, John. *Leadershift: Transitioning from the Pastoral to the Apostolic.* Chicago: Crusaders Ministry, 2000.

———. *Moving in the Apostolic: God's Plan to Lead His Church to the Final Victory.* Ventura, CA: Renew, 1999.

Fee, Gordon D. *The First Epistle to the Corinthians.* Grand Rapids, MI: Eerdmans, 1987.

Ferguson, Everett. "Apostle." In *Encyclopedia of Early Christianity,* edited by Everett Ferguson, 72–73. New York: Garland, 1990.

Gallagher, Robert L., and Paul Hertig, eds. *Mission In Acts: Ancient Narratives in Contemporary Context.* Maryknoll, NY: Orbis, 2004.

Garner, Martin. *A Call for Apostles Today.* Cambridge, UK: Grove, 2007.

Gehring, Roger W. *House Church and Mission: The Importance of Household Structures in Early Christianity.* Peabody, MA: Hendrickson, 2004.

Gibbs, Eddie. *Church NEXT: Quantum Changes in How We Do Ministry.* Downers Grove, IL: InterVarsity, 2000.

Gibbs, Eddie, and Ryan K. Bolger. *Emerging Churches.* Grand Rapids, MI: Baker Academic, 2005.

Graber, F., and D. Muller. "Apostle" In *The New International Dictionary of New Testament Theology,* edited by Colin Brown, 126–35. Vol. 1. Grand Rapids, MI: Zondervan, 1975.

Green, Joel B., and Scott McKnight, eds. *Dictionary of Jesus and the Gospel.* Downers Grove, IL: InterVarsity, 1992.

Grenz, Stanley, and John R. Franke. *Beyond Foundationalism: Shaping Theology in a Postmodern Context.* Louisville, KY: Westminster John Knox, 2001.

Guder, Darrell L. *The Continuing Conversion of the Church.* Grand Rapids, MI: Eerdmans, 2000.

———. "From Mission and Theology to Missional Theology." *Princeton Seminary Bulletin.* NS 24.1 (2003) 36–54.

———, ed. *Missional Church: A Vision for the Sending of the Church in North America.* Grand Rapids, MI: Eerdmans, 1998.

Hall, Douglas John. *Confessing the Faith: Christian Theology in a North American Context.* Minneapolis, MN: Fortress, 1996.

Hammett, John. "An Ecclesiological Assessment of the Emerging Church." *Criswell Theological Review* 3.2 (2006) 29–49.

Hays, Richard B. *Interpretation: First Corinthians.* Louisville, KY: John Knox, 1997.

Hoehner, Harold W. *Ephesians: An Exegetical Commentary.* Grand Rapids, MI: Baker Academic, 2002.

Karkkainen, Veli-Matti. *An Introduction to Ecclesiology: Ecumenical, Historical, and Global Perspectives.* Downers Grove, IL: InterVarsity, 2002.

Kelly, John. *End Time Warriors.* Ventura, CA: Regal, 1999.

Kimball, Dan. *The Emerging Church.* Grand Rapids, MI: Zondervan, 2003.

Kirk, J. Andrew. "Apostleship Since Rengstorf: Towards a Synthesis." *New Testament Studies* 21 (1974) 249–64.

Kreider, Larry. "Dove Christian Fellowship International." In *The New Apostolic Churches,* 103–16. Ventura, CA: Regal, 1998.

Kruse, C. G. "Apostle." In *Dictionary of Jesus and The Gospels,* edited by Joel B. Green, 27–33. Downers Grove, IL: InterVarsity, 1992.

Kung, Hans. *The Church and Ecumenism.* New York: Paulist, 1965.

Liardon, Roberts. "Embassy Christian Center." In *The New Apostolic Churches,* edited by C. Peter Wagner, 117–30. Ventura, CA: Regal, 1998.

BIBLIOGRAPHY

Lincoln, Andrew T. *Ephesians*. Word Biblical Commentary 42. Dallas, TX: Word, 1982.

McGavran, Donald A. *Understanding Church Growth*. Grand Rapids, MI: Eerdmans, 1990.

Meeks, Wayne A. *The First Urban Christians: The Social World of the Apostle Paul*. New Haven, CT: Yale University Press, 1983.

Meier, John P. *Companions and Competitors*. Vol. 3 of *A Marginal Jew*. New York: Doubleday, 1991.

Newbigin, Lesslie. "Missionary Ecclesiology." In *An Introduction to Ecclesiology: Ecumenical, Historical, and Global Perspective*, edited by Veli-Matti Kärkkäinen, 151–59. Downers Grove, IL: Inter Varsity, 2002.

———. *The Open Secret: An Introduction to the Theology of Mission*. Grand Rapids, MI: Eerdmans, 1995.

Patzia, Arthur G. *The Emergence of the Church: Context, Growth, Leadership & Worship*. Downers Grove, IL: Inter Varsity, 2001.

Plummer, Robert L. *Paul's Understanding of the Church's Mission: Did the Apostle Paul Expect the Early Christian Communities to Evangelize?* Eugene, OR: Wipf & Stock, 2006.

Roxburgh, Alan. "What is the Difference between Missional and Emerging Churches?" *TheBolgBlog* (blog), April 2, 2007. https://thebolgblog.typepad.com/thebolgblog/video.

Schnabel, Eckhard. *Jesus and the Twelve*. Vol. 1 of *Early Christian Mission*. Downers Grove, IL: InterVarsity, 2004.

Shenk, Wilbert R. *Changing Frontiers of Mission*. Maryknoll, NY: Orbis, 1993.

Snyder, Howard A., and Daniel V. Runyon. *Decoding the Church: Mapping the DNA of Christ's Body*. Grand Rapids, MI: Baker, 2002.

Stark, Rodney. *The Rise of Christianity: How the Obscure, Marginal Jesus Movement Became the Dominant Religious Force in the Western World in a Few Centuries*. Princeton, NJ: Princeton University Press, 1997.

Talbert, Charles H. *Ephesians and Colossians*. Grand Rapids, MI: Baker Academic, 2007.

Thiselton, Anthony C. *The First Epistle to the Corinthians*. Grand Rapids, MI: Eerdmans, 2000.

Van Engen, Charles. *God's Missionary People: Rethinking the Purpose of the Local Church*. Grand Rapids, MI: Baker, 1991.

———. "Mission Defined and Described." Unpublished manuscript, 2009.

Van Gelder, Craig. *The Essence of the Church: A Community Created by the Spirit*. Grand Rapids, MI: Baker, 2000.

Vander Broek, Lyle D. *Breaking Barriers: The Possibilities of Christian Community in a Lonely World*. Grand Rapids, MI: Brazos, 2002.

Wagner, C. P. *Apostles and Prophets: The Foundation of the Church*. Ventura, CA: Regal, 2000.

———. *Changing Church: How God is Leading His Church Into the Future*. Ventura, CA: Regal, 2004.

———. *Churchquake*. Ventura, CA: Regal, 1999.

———. *The New Apostolic Church*. Ventura, CA: Regal, 1998.

———. *Spheres of Authority: Apostles in Today's Church*. Colorado Springs, CO: Wagner, 2002.

Wright, N. T. *Paul for Everyone: The Prison Letters*. Louisville, KY: Westminster John Knox, 2004.

www.ingramcontent.com/pod-product-compliance
Lightning Source LLC
Chambersburg PA
CBHW062025220426
43662CB00010B/1473